PLANT
POWERED
MEXICAN

PLANT POWERED MEXICAN

Fast, Fresh Recipes from a
Mexican-American Kitchen

KATE RAMOS

HARVARD
COMMON
PRESS

Brimming with creative inspiration, how-to projects, and useful information to enrich your everyday life, Quarto Knows is a favorite destination for those pursuing their interests and passions. Visit our site and dig deeper with our books into your area of interest: Quarto Creates, Quarto Cooks, Quarto Homes, Quarto Lives, Quarto Drives, Quarto Explores, Quarto Gifts, or Quarto Kids.

First Published in 2020 by The Harvard Common Press, an imprint of The Quarto Group, 100 Cummings Center, Suite 265-D, Beverly, MA 01915, USA.
T (978) 282-9590 F (978) 283-2742 QuartoKnows.com

The Harvard Common Press titles are also available at discount for retail, wholesale, promotional, and bulk purchase. For details, contact the Special Sales Manager by email at specialsales@quarto.com or by mail at The Quarto Group, Attn: Special Sales Manager, 100 Cummings Center, Suite 265-D, Beverly, MA 01915, USA.

25 24 23 22 21   1 2 3 4 5

ISBN: 978-0-76037-114-5

Digital edition published in 2021
eISBN: 978-0-76037-115-2

Library of Congress Cataloging-in-Publication Data
Names: Ramos, Kate, author.
Title: Plant powered Mexican / Kate Ramos.
Description: Beverly, MA, USA : Fair Winds Press, 2021. | Includes index. |
   Summary: "Plant Powered Mexican goes far beyond veggie tacos, delivering
   creative recipes from Al Pastor Winter Squash to Jackfruit Tinga Grain
   Bowls"-- Provided by publisher.
Identifiers: LCCN 2021022633 (print) | LCCN 2021022634 (ebook) | ISBN
   9780760371145 | ISBN 9780760371152 (eISBN)
Subjects: LCSH: Cooking, Mexican. | Vegetarian cooking. | Cooking (Natural
   foods) | LCGFT: Cookbooks.
Classification: LCC TX715 .R213278 2021 (print) | LCC TX715 (ebook) | DDC
   641.5972--dc23
LC record available at https://lccn.loc.gov/2021022633

LC ebook record available at https://lccn.loc.gov/2021022634

Design: Tanya R. Jacobson
Photography: Kate Ramos

Printed in China

TO ARMANDO

A todo dar mi amor.

CONTENTS

....

INTRODUCTION

● ●

I'LL BE THE FIRST TO ADMIT I DID NOT GROW UP EATING MEXICAN FOOD OR PLANT-BASED MEALS. I WAS, HOWEVER, BORN A COOK . . . AND, MORE THAN THAT, AN INQUISITIVE FOOD-LOVER.

I consider myself one of the lucky ones who stumbles into their passion early. In my case, I found it at around ten years old and never looked back. It came as a surprise to no one that at twenty-one I was a sous chef at Mustards Grill in Napa Valley. I mean I *had* been cooking for more than a decade by then.

Truth be told, I was in way over my head. It was only the generosity of my fellow cooks and my newfound love for Mexican cuisine that kept me going. Well, that and meeting a handsome young man, Armando, who would become my husband.

I still remember the lunches and dinners I shared with my coworkers in the back of the restaurant kitchen, plates hovered over our knees as we perched on overturned milk crates. It was there that I first tried chilaquiles, had my first ethereal spoonful of mole, inhaled the fragrant steam of pozole, and tasted my first fluffy bites of tamales fresh from the steamer.

Growing up in Iowa, I had never had these foods or even knew about them, and as a curious cook I was mesmerized. A whole new world of flavor was opening. When Armando and I got married and I became part of his Mexican-American family, I was fully and deeply committed to learning everything I could about this beautiful cuisine. Mexican food is so diverse, complex, and sophisticated. It is something you can explore for a lifetime and always find more to discover. It is a mosaic of native ingredients and worldly influences

that varies depending on location and climate. It is vibrant and alive, and it stirs my soul like nothing else.

With this book I hope to capture at least a hint of that spirit, and I've done my best to pour my passion for Mexican cuisine into these pages. That doesn't mean every recipe in here is authentically Mexican. Many recipes use Mexican ingredients in dishes that reflect my family's SoCal lifestyle or speak to my midwestern roots.

The beauty of these flavors is they move so seamlessly to bring new life to everyday dishes and they are perfect for those who enjoy a plant-based diet or simply love vegetables. That brings me to the other purpose of this book. We're eating and cooking differently today because the world has changed. Swapping out a meat-based meal for a vegetarian one is a good idea for our health as people and the health of our planet as well.

My family doesn't exclusively eat vegetarian meals, but we have cut back our meat consumption considerably over the years. When Armando and I were newlyweds, a romantic steak dinner was the norm. That meant a steak for each of us—which seems insane now. As a family of four, when we eat steak these days we share one New York strip. We're eating meat more as a condiment; it adds a bit of fat and flavor that enhances the real star of the show: the vegetables!

The way we choose to eat matters. What we put on our plates will affect the world our children and grandchildren inhabit. And it pleases me to no end that so many of us are doing something about it. We are growing our own veggies, becoming regulars at our local farmers' markets, and investing in Community Supported Agriculture (CSA) boxes at rapidly growing rates. But the biggest challenge I hear from so many of my blog's readers is, "Okay, I have these beautiful vegetables. Now what? How do I make it a meal my whole family will eat?"

As you flip through these pages, I hope you'll find many recipes to inspire you to try something different. Make a trip to your local Latin market, or try a new ingredient. You may even find yourself inspired to get lost in the rich world of Mexican cooking just like I was all those years ago.

I
MY PANTRY

MY FAMILY HAS LIVED ALL OVER THE UNITED STATES, FROM CALIFORNIA TO NORTH DAKOTA WITH A FEW STOPS IN BETWEEN—SO I KNOW HOW CHALLENGING IT CAN BE TO FIND THE MEXICAN INGREDIENTS THAT MAKE THE DIFFERENCE BETWEEN GOOD MEXICAN FOOD AND GREAT MEXICAN FOOD. EVEN HERE IN SOUTHERN CALIFORNIA, A FEW HOURS FROM THE MEXICAN BORDER, I CAN HAVE A TOUGH TIME FINDING HOJA SANTA OR FRESH REQUESÓN CHEESE.

My first piece of advice is to find your nearest Latin market and make it a regular stop in your weekly shopping trips. There is a good chance you will find everything you need to make the recipes in this book, and you may also walk away with perfectly ripe avocados, the freshest cilantro, homemade tortillas, and other delights. (As my kids can tell you, our local store has the best paletas.)

If a trip to a Latin market is not in your future, the next best place to find those hard-to-find Mexican ingredients is the internet. If you come up short, I've tried to include substitutes for not-so-common ingredients when I feel the substitution won't change the dish all that much.

In this chapter, I will share a peek into my pantry essentials. It doesn't encompass the full spectrum of Mexican ingredients, but instead focuses on the things you'll need to make the recipes in this book. These are the staples I use to make our family's meals. This book won't go into complex dishes such as tamales or ask you to make your own tortillas—although if you love Mexican food, I highly suggest giving it a try! Here we'll rely on high-quality, powerful ingredients to bring the best Mexican flavors to your table in record time.

SALTS, SPICES, AND HERBS

Knowing how to season your cooking with salt is the single most important skill a cook can master. Salt heightens the flavor of everything it touches, but it can also ruin a dish if used with a heavy hand. Using the right salt is also important. These are my go-to salts and spices.

Kosher Salt

Kosher salt has larger crystals than table salt; I find it better for most uses because they dissolve more slowly. Kosher salt is less salty by weight and I find the flakes are easier to distribute than the fine texture of table salt.

Getting comfortable with how a salt feels is important because different brands of kosher salt have different shapes and sizes of salt crystals. You'll want to learn how much salt is enough by using your fingers, not a measuring spoon; a teaspoon of one brand may be saltier than a teaspoon of another.

Two common brands of kosher salt are Morton and Diamond Crystal. Most professional kitchens and cooks use Diamond Crystal because it has a flakier texture and is less salty. I prefer Morton and it is what I used to create the recipes in this book. I like its bigger, coarser grains and saltier punch.

That said, the best salt for you to master is the one you use the most—so you can be consistent. With a little practice, a pinch of salt will be the same today as it is tomorrow. Measure the salt with your fingers and taste as you go to become a more confident and skilled cook.

Flaky Sea Salt

Large, thin flakes of sea salt are perfect for finishing a dish. My favorite, and probably the most well-known brand, is Maldon. Reach for this salt when you want to add a final touch of clean, pure salinity and a bit of crunch.

Tajín

Tajín (pronounced Ta-HEEN) is a chile-lime salt from Guadalajara, Mexico. It is such a beloved spice you can now find it in many grocery stores. Most commonly used to add a kick to fresh-cut fruit and cocktail glass rims, Tajín's special blend of chiles, lime, and salt should hold a permanent spot on your kitchen counter.

Sal de Gusano

This traditional Oaxacan salt is flavored with toasted and ground maguey worms, which are not technically worms but caterpillars of a butterfly commonly known as the tequila giant skipper. The salt (which typically also has a touch of ground chile) has a unique umami and sweet agave flavor and illuminates everything it touches.

Epazote

Available fresh or dried, epazote is a pungent, lemony herb that is commonly added to beans to make their "digestive effects" less potent. It has a distinctive flavor of mint meets lemon meets dried salted plum that mellows as it cooks. In a pinch, oregano can be substituted.

Mexican Oregano

I started growing Mexican oregano in my garden mainly because I use it so often, I got tired of having to go to the store. It is distinct from the more common Mediterranean varieties of oregano because it's not in the oregano (*Origanum*) family at all. Mexican oregano is in the same family as verbena and has that same citrusy, floral flavor. You can still substitute "regular" Mediterranean oregano, but it will have a different flavor.

Achiote Paste

Achiote paste is a bright red *recado*, or blend of different spices, most commonly used in the Yucatán. The vibrant color and tart flavor come from achiote or annatto seeds. Bricks of achiote paste can often be found with the other Latin ingredients in most large supermarkets.

Ceylon Cinnamon

Also known as canela or true cinnamon, this is the variety of cinnamon most commonly used in Mexican cooking. It is much softer than cassia cinnamon (the one found in most stores in the United States). It looks and feels like tough leather and has a warm, sweet, mellow flavor.

GROUND CHILE POWDERS

●●●●●●●●●●●●●●●●●●●●●●●●●●●●●●●

The generic chili powder you find in most grocery stores is actually a mixture of different ground dried chiles and spices, like cumin and coriander. There's nothing wrong with it; I often keep a jar on my spice rack to add a quick spice mix to beans. However, if you are looking for the pure flavor of a particular chile, look for powders made from only one type. A few of my favorites follow.

Guajillo Chile Powder

This mild vibrant red chile powder is made from ground guajillo chiles. These slightly sour chiles are widely used throughout Mexico and add a unique earthy-sweet flavor with a touch of tang at the end. The ground chile powder is an easy way to incorporate their special flavor without the need for toasting or soaking.

Substitution: ground ancho chile powder or mild chili powder

Arbol Chile Powder

The spicy stuff! This is the chile powder you reach for when you want to add some heat. Arbol chiles have a unique nuttiness with a potent kick. The ground powder is excellent for sprinkling over a finished dish for a spicy touch.

Substitution: cayenne powder

Ancho Chile Powder

Ancho chiles are the dried version of poblano peppers and have a medium spiciness level and dark, dried-fruit flavor. Ancho chile powder is one of the most widely available ground chile powders so it should be easy to find this one.

Habanero Chile Powder

For spice-lovers only: this is set-your-mouth-on-fire hot, but it's so good in small amounts. Habaneros are mainly used in Yucatecan cooking and are typically balanced out with something sweet. I like to mix the chile powder with salt for sprinkling over warm Homemade Tortilla Chips (page 167).

MAGIC SPICE MIX!

INGREDIENTS

- 1 tablespoon (6 g) guajillo chile powder
- 1 teaspoon kosher salt
- ½ teaspoon ground black pepper
- ½ teaspoon smoked paprika
- ½ teaspoon garlic powder
- ½ teaspoon ground coriander
- ½ teaspoon dried epazote (page 14) or oregano (preferably Mexican)

MAKES ENOUGH FOR 1 TO 2 RECIPES

(about 2 tablespoons [10 g])

This slightly smoky spice mix adds a bit of magic to anything it touches. I use it to season everything from picadillo (page 79) to fajitas (page 128). Mix up a batch and keep it in a jar on your spice rack for impromptu boosts of flavor.

❀ INSTRUCTIONS ❀

Mix all the ingredients together in a small bowl until evenly combined. Use immediately or keep in a tightly sealed container at room temperature for up to 1 month. I keep leftover spice jars handy for just this purpose.

HOT SAUCE

I'm not here to tell you which bottled Mexican hot sauce is the best. It is a very personal decision, and everyone has their favorite! They all have varying degrees of heat and acid. My husband prefers Cholula while I'm a Valentina kind of gal. We keep our pantry stocked with both; it's the secret to our happy marriage.

FRESH AND DRIED CHILES

Poblano

These large, forest green peppers are usually mild and grassy, but just when you think you will bite into something tame, a fiery one will jump up and get you. The hotter and drier the growing conditions, the spicier the pepper will be. If you are heat sensitive, take a small bite out of the pepper before cooking with it.

Jalapeño

Jalapeños are the most popular of the fresh green chiles and can be found in any grocery store. They are a good alternative if you can't find serrano or Fresno chiles.

Serrano

Serrano chiles look like smaller, skinnier jalapeños, and they prove that the smaller the chile the spicier it will be. Through the heat, serranos have an intense floral flavor that is irresistible.

Fresno

Fresno chiles are the only one on this list that are not traditionally Mexican. They were cultivated in the 1950s in Fresno County, California. They often are mistaken for ripe jalapeños, but they are their own chile pepper. They are milder than a jalapeño, with thinner walls and bright red skin. They can be hard to find outside of California. Substitute jalapeños, just use less.

Dried Pasilla Chiles

Fresh chilaca chiles are dried and become burgundy-colored pasilla chiles, which are medium-hot, rich, and slightly bitter—not at all sweet.

Dried Arbol Chiles

Tiny, skinny, and spicy, these dried, pencil-thin chiles pack a punch.

Dried Chipotle Chiles

Chipotle chiles are the name given to ripe jalapeños that have been smoked and dried. Due to their thick flesh, jalapeños have the tendency to get moldy when they air-dry, so smoking them has always been the preferred method of preservation.

Dried Chiltepín Chiles

Chiltepín chiles are round, tiny chiles that resemble puffed up pink peppercorns. They are fiery and, unlike other dried chiles, they are best used chopped and sprinkled on top of a dish rather than used to make sauces. If you can't find them, use arbol chiles or even crushed red chile flakes.

Dried Guajillo Chiles

Guajillo chiles are the most beloved of all the dried chiles mostly because their rustic, sweet, mild flavor goes well with just about anything. These long chiles with smooth skin are the dried form of the mirasol chile. They can be found in most grocery stores in the Latin food aisle.

Dried Ancho Chiles

The dried form of poblano peppers is called *ancho* because they are wide. They are also wrinkled, chewy, and great for when you want a deep chile flavor with dark undertones yet mild to medium spice.

CHIPOTLE PEPPERS IN ADOBO

●●●●●●●●●●●●●●●●●●●●●●●●●●●●●●●●●●●●●

Canned chipotles in adobo are the dried chipotles that have been rehydrated and packed in adobo sauce ready to use. What is adobo sauce you might ask? Adobo sauce is a mild chile sauce made with lots of garlic and vinegar. It is excellent on its own but gives the chipotles a boost of tang as well.

MEXICAN CHEESES

Queso Fresco

Queso fresco translates to "fresh cheese." It is soft and pillowy and is typically a cow's milk cheese. It adds a silky crumble and mellow note to spicy tacos, chilaquiles, enchiladas, and enmoladas (page 71). It is used most often to finish dishes, although it does make an excellent quesadilla.

Queso fresco doesn't have a good substitute. The closest thing would be feta, but it is much stronger in flavor.

Cotija

The opposite side of the spectrum from queso fresco is Cotija cheese. An aged cow's milk cheese, it is dry, salty, and crumbly. It is used as a garnish, but you'll want to use it anywhere you're looking to add a salty kick, from a bowl of beans to elote (page 63). Parmesan can be substituted, but Cotija has a cleaner flavor.

Queso Oaxaca

Queso Oaxaca (also known as quesillo) is a mild, stringy cheese that melts beautifully and has a buttery flavor. It is most commonly sold in sticks (like string cheese) or in ropes wrapped into a ball shape. Mozzarella makes a fine substitute.

Requesón

Requesón is Mexico's equivalent of ricotta cheese, so soft and luxurious it melts in your mouth. Instead of being made from curds like most cheese, requesón is made with whey. It is used as a filling for empanadas and in dips and sauces as well as a finishing touch to dishes that need a hint of creaminess. Try it in the Grilled Vegetable Salad with Herbed Requesón and Citrus Vinaigrette (page 131). Ricotta can be substituted.

Panela

Panela is made from skim milk, giving it a firm and flexible texture. It will not melt when heated, which is why it's awesome for grilling (like in the Queso Asado on page 138). It has a mild flavor and smooth texture.

Mexican Crema

There are many varieties of Mexican cremas available at most Latin markets. I encourage you to try them all to see which one you like best. My favorites are crema Mexicana or table cream, which is like very thick heavy cream with just the slightest bit of tang, and crema agria, which is more sour, like a mix between American sour cream and crème fraîche.

CORN

Pozole/Hominy

In Mexico, pozole refers to a specific type of field corn grown to use in its namesake soup. This corn is almost impossible to find outside of Mexico, so often pozole soup is made with hominy—hard dent or field corn that has been nixtamalized (soaked in calcium hydroxide) until it is soft and chewy. Canned hominy is easily found in any grocery store. You can also find dried hominy and presoaked hominy in many Latin markets.

Masa Harina

Corn masa flour, or *masa harina*, is not the same as cornmeal. It is the flour made from ground nixtamalized corn and is used in place of fresh masa dough to make everything from tortillas to sopes (page 65) to tamales and masa dumplings (page 85). It is widely available in most grocery stores next to the all-purpose flour and baking supplies.

A WORD ON OIL

Many of my recipes call for olive oil, which is not the most typical oil used in Mexico but reflects my SoCal way of cooking. I've come to enjoy many of these recipes with those flavors.

While it is not common, olive oil production is happening in Mexico, mostly in Baja's Valle de Guadalupe. This bright, sunny olive oil is popping up on some store shelves and can be bought online. It is definitely worth searching out.

Avocado oil is also becoming more available and is universally suited for Mexican cooking. It has a high smoke point and is fairly mild. I use avocado oil when I don't want the flavor of olive oil to come through. It is healthier for you than canola or vegetable oil and works equally well for salad dressings as it does for frying, grilling, or roasting. If you can't find avocado oil, sunflower oil is a good substitute.

OTHER INGREDIENTS

Jamaica Flowers

Dried Jamaica (hibiscus) flowers are not flowers at all but the outer covering that encloses the hibiscus petals before the flower blooms. Their astringent, floral flavor is most popular in drinks such as Agua de Jamaica (page 181), but they can also be rehydrated and eaten as in the sopes filling on page 65. They are pricey everywhere but the Latin market, which sells overflowing bins of them for next to nothing.

Tamarind

Tamarind can be found as sour-sweet brown pods that look like oversized string beans. The tree is not native to Mexico but was brought by the Spanish and is now part of Mexican gastronomy in the form of candy, drinks, and other sweets. Look for it in paste form in Latin markets if you're making recipes such as the tamarind sauce on page 148.

Duritos

Duritos de harina (also known as chicharrones de harina) are the addictive, crunchy wheat chip in ever-adorable wheel shapes, sold by street vendors all over Mexico. When you buy a bag, the vendor douses them in lime juice and generously sprinkles them with tongue-tingling spice mix, then holds the bag closed and shakes vigorously until they are completely coated.

Most Latin markets sell bags of fried duritos or you can buy the uncooked wheels and fry them yourself (there's a recipe for that on my blog). They make a delicious snack and are also delightful garnish when crumbled. Sprinkle wherever you need something crunchy.

Piloncillo

These cone or rectangular-shaped blocks of raw, unrefined sugar are the sweetener in many traditional Mexican desserts and an essential in the Mexican pantry for everything from sweets to drinks to some salsas (page 69). You can substitute dark brown sugar for piloncillo. They are not exactly the same, but they both have a strong molasses flavor.

Amaranth

Amaranth has been used in Mexican cooking since the Aztecs began cultivating it more than 8,000 years ago. Amaranth is high in protein and loaded with vitamins. It's a superfood addition to oatmeal, salads, and garnishes for soups (like on page 39 [Chilled Avocado Soup with Farmers' Market Fairy Dust]). Popped amaranth is ready to eat and can be found next to the dried beans in most Latin markets.

Pumpkin Seeds/Pepitas

Guess what? All pumpkin seeds are not pepitas! If you've ever roasted your Halloween jack-o'-lantern pumpkin seeds, you may be wondering why they don't look like the ones you buy from the store. The gray-green seeds labeled pepitas are grown without the white covering of a hull you typically find on most pumpkin seeds. Certain types of pumpkins produce their seeds this way, and these, my friends, are pepitas.

EQUIPMENT

Comal

The workhorse of a Mexican kitchen is the comal. Traditional comales are a flat ceramic stone that can resist the high flame of an open fire, but most today are made of cast iron. That means if you don't have a comal, you can use a good ol' cast-iron skillet.

What do you do with a comal? Char vegetables. Toast dried chiles, seeds, and nuts. Warm tortillas . . . in our house, we even make toast on it. Our comal sits on our stove all day every day—that's how much we use it. If you love Mexican cooking, I highly suggest investing in one. They aren't that expensive, and you will get your money's worth.

Molcajete

Many tools used by traditional cooks in Mexico are impractical for most of us to use daily in our kitchens. (I can only dream to have the strength to grind corn for tortillas on a metate.) However, the one tool I do use often is a molcajete and tejolote, the Mexican volcanic stone version of a mortar and pestle. Do you need to have this to make the recipes in this book? No. But when you want your salsa to be not completely smooth—but more pureed than chopped—the molcajete will do the trick.

If you buy a new molcajete, first, make sure it is made from volcanic rock and not some knock-off made from concrete that will always leave grit in your salsa. Next, clean and season it before you use it for the first time: Add a handful of dried rice to the molcajete and grind it into a powder with the tejolote. The rice will soak up any bits of stone or dirt on the molcajete. Dump out the ground rice and wipe clean with a towel. Smash some garlic, cilantro, and chiles in the molcajete into a paste and leave overnight. Clean out the next day and you'll be ready to go!

2

LOW COOK

WRITING A BOOK ABOUT VEGETABLES MEANS CELEBRATING THEIR INTRINSIC BEAUTY. WHAT BETTER WAY TO DO THAT THAN TO CREATE RECIPES USING VEGETABLES IN THEIR MOST BASIC FORM?

These no- and low-cook recipes are perfect for blazing hot summer nights when you can't imagine heating up the kitchen or when you need something super fast. But even more, this chapter is for when you find yourself in possession of the most excellent tomato, an ideal avocado, or the crispiest cucumber.

I want you to explore all sorts of vegetables and fruits, not just in summer when the easy-to-love beauties are calling your name. There are ideas in this chapter to help you dive into every season in that vibrant, breezy way Mexican ingredients invite us to do.

And we're not just talking all salads either. There are easy chilled soups, a generous sandwich (page 39), aguachile (page 51), and—everyone's favorite—avocado toast (page 52). And yes, there are salads of all sorts: a fall salad with pomegranate and persimmon (page 37), a winter Caesar with hunks of chile-laced squash (page 47), and a colorful rainbow salad (page 43) that has become so popular at our house, we just call it "The Salad." These recipes are intended to be the main event and they also make excellent sides for a more robust meal.

Welcome to the dynamic, addictive world of bright, fresh Mexican flavors.

MEXICAN GAZPACHO WITH CHOPPED CUCUMBER SALAD

INGREDIENTS

FOR THE GAZPACHO

- 2 pounds (907 g) ripest most flavorful tomatoes you can find, cored and roughly chopped
- ½ cup (118 ml) extra-virgin olive oil
- 1½ teaspoons salt
- 1 teaspoon granulated sugar
- 1 (6-inch, or 15-cm) piece baguette, preferably day-old bread
- 2 tablespoons (28 ml) red wine vinegar
- 2 small cucumbers, chopped
- 1 medium poblano pepper corded, seeded, and chopped
- 1 clove garlic
- 1 teaspoon ground cumin
- ¼ cup (60 ml) Valentina hot sauce

FOR THE CUCUMBER SALAD

- 1 cup (135 g) finely diced English cucumber
- ½ cup (64 g) minced red onion
- ¼ cup (40 g) seeded and minced jalapeño
- 1 tablespoon (15 ml) fresh lime juice (from 1 lime)
- 1 tablespoon (15 ml) extra-virgin olive oil
- ½ teaspoon kosher salt, plus more to taste
- 1 tablespoon (8 g) white sesame seeds
- ¼ teaspoon ground coriander

SERVES 4

In high school I was an exchange student in Andalucía, Spain, the home of gazpacho. There I tasted my first bowl of this silky, chilled tomato soup. A good gazpacho should be bursting with fresh tomato flavor and perfectly smooth with almost a fluffy mouthfeel—this comes from generous amounts of extra-virgin olive oil.

This Mexican version uses the same technique as they do in Spain but with the addition of grassy poblano peppers, cumin, and my favorite hot sauce—Valentina. If you can find Mexican extra-virgin olive oil, that would make a nice touch too. It is becoming more widely available in the United States.

❈ INSTRUCTIONS ❈

To make the gazpacho: In a large bowl, toss the tomatoes with oil, salt, and sugar. Leave to macerate at room temperature for at least 30 minutes or up to 4 hours—the longer the better.

Remove the crust from the baguette and dice into large pieces. Place in a separate bowl and sprinkle with the vinegar. Toss to combine. Set aside to soak up the vinegar while the tomatoes are macerating.

Once the tomatoes are swimming in juice and the bread is moist, add the two mixtures to a blender along with the remaining gazpacho ingredients. Blend until very smooth. Transfer to a container, cover, and chill until cold, at least 2 hours.

Meanwhile, to make the cucumber salad: Combine all the ingredients in a medium bowl. Taste and add more salt, if needed.

Serve the gazpacho in shallow bowls with a scoop of cucumber salad on top.

TECHNIQUE

● ●

One important step makes all the difference between ho-hum gazpacho and ethereal gazpacho. Leave the tomatoes to macerate in the oil, salt, and sugar for as long as 4 hours at room temperature. This brings out all the flavorful juices and aromas of the tomatoes and those juices become the base of the soup.

CAULIFLOWER, PEPITA, AND RICE SALAD LETTUCE WRAPS

INGREDIENTS

- 2 cups (316 g) cooked jasmine rice
- 2 cups (226 g) riced cauliflower
- 2 scallions, minced
- 2 medium red Fresno chile or jalapeno (1 minced, 1 sliced for garnish [optional])
- ½ cup (60 g) diced zucchini
- ½ cup (112 g) pomegranate arils
- ½ cup (24 g) thinly sliced fresh basil, plus a few more whole leaves for garnish
- ¼ cup (35 g) roasted, salted pepitas
- 1 tablespoon (20 g) honey
- 2 tablespoons (28 ml) lime juice
- ¼ cup (59 ml) olive oil
- 1 clove garlic, minced
- ½ teaspoon kosher salt
- ¼ teaspoon ground black pepper
- 1 large head butter lettuce, leaves separated

SERVES 4

●●●●●●●●●●●●●●●

Sunny, crunchy, and fresh, these lettuce wraps are an excellent way to use leftover steamed rice. I particularly love the textural contrast between the tender rice, crunchy cauliflower, and snap of the butter lettuce, but you can make it low carb by using all riced cauliflower instead of the jasmine rice and cauliflower combo.

❈ INSTRUCTIONS ❈

Combine the rice, cauliflower, scallions, minced Fresno chile, zucchini, pomegranate, basil, and pepitas in a large bowl.

In a medium bowl, combine the honey, lime juice, oil, garlic, salt, and black pepper. Whisk until smooth. Pour the dressing over the rice mixture. Toss until well combined and coated in the dressing.

Spoon several tablespoons of the cauliflower rice salad into the center of a lettuce leaf, taco-style. Top with sliced Fresno chiles and basil leaves and serve.

PERSIMMON POMEGRANATE CRUNCH SALAD WITH JALAPEÑO VINAIGRETTE

INGREDIENTS

- 1 small head red cabbage, thinly sliced
- 2 Fuyu persimmons, cored, cut in half, and thinly sliced into half-moons (seeds removed if there are any)
- 1 cup (224 g) pomegranate arils
- 2 cups (32 g) fresh cilantro (tender leaves and stems)
- 3 tablespoons (45 ml) vegetable or avocado oil
- 3 tablespoons (45 ml) unseasoned rice vinegar
- 3 scallions, trimmed and minced
- 1 medium jalapeño, stemmed and minced (seeds removed if you'd like it less spicy)
- ½ teaspoon kosher salt, plus more to taste
- A few pinches of ground black pepper

SERVES 4

I suppose this is a slaw of sorts—not a happenstance, throw-on-top-of-a-taco slaw though. It's one that takes more intention and tenderness and one that is immensely satisfying and full of fall ingredients.

As a girl who loves texture, I must say this salad is so up my alley. It's a mouth workout and has a sweet, tangy, spicy profile that makes it a completely acceptable light dinner or lunch. To make it more substantial, add a few shavings of aged white Cheddar or a sprinkling of cooked chickpeas, or serve it alongside the Queso Asado and Calabacitas (page 138). This is a good, make-ahead salad for picnics or potlucks; you can make it up to an hour in advance!

❈ INSTRUCTIONS ❈

Toss the cabbage, persimmons, pomegranate arils, and cilantro in a large serving bowl. Season with salt and pepper, and give it another toss.

In a separate small bowl or mason jar, combine the oil, vinegar, scallions, jalapeño, and salt. Whisk until well combined; or if using a mason jar, cover with a lid and shake.

Drizzle the dressing over the salad, and toss to coat well. Taste and add more salt and pepper, if needed.

Continued >

POWER-UP
YOUR FRUIT

●●●●●●●●●●●●●●●●●●●●●●●●●●●●●●●●●●●●●●

Persimmons are so nutrient dense! The saying should
be a persimmon a day keeps the doctor away, not
the apple—especially when it comes to heart disease.
These gorgeous orange fruits are loaded with fiber and
antioxidants. The two most common types are Fuyu
and Hachiya persimmons. The squat, donut-shaped
Fuyu persimmons are the ones you want to use for this
salad. They are sweet and edible when still crisp with
texture like an apple. The Hachiya persimmons are not
sweet until they become soft, almost falling apart.
They are best used in baked goods or eaten raw
with a spoon.

CHILLED AVOCADO SOUP WITH FARMERS' MARKET FAIRY DUST

Hands down, this is my sister-in-law's favorite recipe in the whole entire book. We have an enormous avocado tree in our backyard, and in the summer I whip up this chilled soup whenever she comes over. It is as refreshing as can be, with lots of juicy cucumber and lime to balance out the richness of the avocado. Plus, it couldn't get more beautiful. Especially with a garnish that adds a bit of crunch and a sprinkling of flower petals so glorious you feel like it was touched with fairy dust.

Look for edible flowers at the farmers' market. Those petals are the least likely to have been sprayed. Or grow your own! Edible flowers such as nasturtiums and marigolds grow like weeds in almost any climate.

Continued >

INGREDIENTS

FOR THE SOUP

- 1 large, ripe avocado, peeled and pitted
- 2 cups (475 ml) cold water
- 2 small Persian cucumbers, chopped
- 2 scallions, trimmed and chopped
- 1 serrano chile, stemmed and chopped
- ¼ cup (60 ml) fresh lime juice (from 2 limes)
- ¼ cup (4 g) chopped fresh cilantro (tender leaves and stems)
- ¼ cup (59 ml) olive oil
- 1 teaspoon kosher salt

FOR THE FAIRY DUST

- ¼ cup (36 g) roasted, salted sunflower seeds
- ¼ cup (36 g) white sesame seeds
- ¼ cup (8 g) popped amaranth
- ¼ cup (14 g) fresh edible flower petals, such as nasturtiums, pansies, marigolds, or cornflowers
- 1 teaspoon toasted cumin seeds

SERVES 4

●●●●●●●●●●●●●●●●

❀ INSTRUCTIONS ❀

To make the soup: Add the avocado, water, cucumbers, scallions, chile, lime juice, cilantro, oil, and salt to a blender. Blend until smooth. Chill until completely cold.

To make the fairy dust: Add the sunflower seeds, sesame seeds, amaranth, flowers, and cumin seeds to a small bowl. Mix gently.

Ladle the cold soup into bowls and sprinkle the fairy dust over the top.

RED LEAF RAINBOW SALAD WITH CRISPY TORTILLA STRIPS AND MANGO DRESSING

INGREDIENTS

FOR THE DRESSING

- 2 tablespoons (32 g) mango chutney
- ¼ cup (60 ml) fresh lime juice (from 2 limes)
- 2 tablespoons (30 ml) olive oil
- 2 tablespoons (15 g) minced scallions
- ½ teaspoon kosher salt
- Pinch of cayenne powder

FOR THE TORTILLA STRIPS

- 4 (4- to 6-inch, or 10- to 15-cm) corn tortillas
- ⅔ cup (158 ml) avocado or sunflower oil
- A few pinches of kosher salt

FOR THE SALAD

- 1 small head red leaf lettuce, torn into bite-sized pieces
- 1 cup (124 g) red cherry tomatoes, halved
- 1 large carrot, sliced into thin strips
- 1 medium yellow bell pepper, cored and sliced into thin strips
- 1 cup (70 g) shredded purple cabbage

SERVES 4

This salad is for my farmers' market friends. If you are a farmers' market regular, I'm talking to you! Think of buying the ingredients for this salad like a treasure hunt, tracking down an ingredient, no matter the season, that fits into a color of the rainbow. This is particularly fun for kids. Red could be sweet bell peppers, crunchy radishes, or even pomegranate seeds in the winter. Orange can be carrots, but use your imagination; tomatoes are also orange in the summer and so is squash or sweet potatoes in the fall and winter months. You get the picture! I've listed my favorite summer combination here.

❈ INSTRUCTIONS ❈

To make the dressing: Combine all the dressing ingredients in a mason jar. Shake vigorously until well combined. Set aside.

To make the tortilla strips: Slice the tortillas into ¼-inch (6-mm)-thick strips. Heat the oil in a medium frying pan over medium heat. Dip one strip into the oil; if bubbles immediately surround the strip, it is hot enough to fry. If not, give it 1 to 2 minutes to heat up.

Add the in two batches to the hot oil. Stir gently with metal tongs until they are golden brown and very crispy, about 2 to 3 minutes. Remove to a paper towel–lined plate and sprinkle with salt. Repeat with the second batch.

To make the salad: Arrange all the ingredients on a large platter. Lay the tortilla strips over the top, and drizzle with the dressing.

WINTER-IN-BAJA DETOX BOWL

INGREDIENTS

- 2 medium ruby red grapefruit
- ¼ cup (7.5 g) chopped fresh mint
- ¼ cup (4 g) chopped fresh cilantro (tender leaves and stems)
- 2 tablespoons (30 ml) extra-virgin olive oil
- 1 tablespoon (3 g) chopped fresh Thai basil or Italian basil
- 1 tablespoon (8 g) white sesame seeds
- 1 teaspoon minced fresh ginger
- ½ teaspoon kosher salt
- 4 medium tomatillos, husks removed, rinsed, and chopped (about 8 ounces [397 g])
- 1 large sweet apple, such as Pink Lady, peeled, cored, and chopped
- 1 large, ripe avocado, peeled, pitted, and chopped

SERVES 2

All of Mexico holds such treasures, but I've got a special place in my heart for Baja. I think because it feels so much like home. From the landscape to the climate to the food, being a Californian doesn't end at the border.

This bowl is full of fresh ingredients such as juicy grapefruit, herbs, and creamy avocado: all things that come straight from Baja. It has so much crunch and bright flavor it will rejuvenate you through the darkest of winters. Eat as is when you need a reset, or add steamed grains if you want more substance.

❈ INSTRUCTIONS ❈

Cut the grapefruit into supremes (see note on page 46) and squeeze the juice into a small bowl. Add the mint, cilantro, oil, basil, sesame seeds, ginger, and salt to the grapefruit juice. Stir to combine.

Divide the grapefruit segments, tomatillos, apples, and avocado among two bowls. Drizzle the dressing over the top and serve.

Continued ⟩

TECHNIQUE

● ●

The trick to getting tender, toothsome pieces of grapefruit or any citrus is to cut them into supremes. Slice the top and bottom off the grapefruit so they sit flat on the cutting board without rolling. Trim away the skin and the white pith by starting at the top and slicing downwards following the curve of the fruit. Try to do this without taking too much of the fruit. If you miss a spot, go back and trim it off when you have removed all the skin.

Hold the grapefruit over a bowl to catch the juices and remove the segments with a paring knife by sliding the knife between one segment and the tough membrane that holds it in place. Repeat on the other side of the segment, then let the segment fall into the bowl. Repeat with all the segments on both grapefruit.

When you have removed all the segments, squeeze the leftover membrane into the bowl to get all the juice out. Remove the grapefruit segments from the bowl and cut into 2 to 3 bite-sized pieces each.

KALE CAESAR SALAD WITH ROASTED KABOCHA SQUASH AND CROUTONS

Despite its Italian ingredients, Caesar salad is as Mexican as mole. It was first created in Tijuana by an Italian immigrant named Caesar Cardini who had moved to Mexico in the early 1920s to avoid Prohibition. You can still visit Caesar's today and order the famed salad, which I highly suggest the next time you find yourself in Tijuana. The restaurant is now run by one of my favorite Mexican chefs, Javier Plascencia, and is definitely worth a visit.

My version strays from Caesar's original creation made with anchovies, Worcestershire sauce, and raw egg, and turns it into a completely plant-powered stunner of a salad. This is my go-to cold-weather main course salad. It's hearty, creamy, cheesy, with chewy kale, roasted kabocha squash, avocado, and plenty of croutons.

Continued >

INGREDIENTS

- ¼ cup (60 g) mayonnaise
- 2 tablespoons (28 ml) fresh lemon juice
- 2 tablespoons (10 g) finely grated Parmesan
- 2 tablespoons (8 g) minced fresh Italian parsley
- 1 clove garlic, minced
- 1 teaspoon Dijon mustard
- ½ teaspoon kosher salt, plus more to taste
- ½ teaspoon ground black pepper, plus more to taste
- 1 large head Tuscan or curly kale, tough stems removed and torn into bite-sized pieces
- ½ recipe Roasted Kabocha Squash (page 171)
- 1 cup (30 g) croutons
- 1 large, ripe avocado, peeled, pitted, and quartered
- ½ cup (40 g) shaved Parmesan

SERVES 4

● ● ● ● ● ● ● ● ● ● ● ● ● ● ●

❊ INSTRUCTIONS ❊

Combine the mayonnaise, lemon juice, Parmesan, parsley, garlic, mustard, salt, and black pepper in a small bowl. Whisk until smooth. Taste and add more salt and pepper, if needed.

Place the kale in a large bowl. Drizzle the dressing over the top and toss to coat, massaging the dressing into the kale with your fingers. It's a messy but a necessary step.

Arrange the kale on a large serving platter. Top with the squash, croutons, avocado, and Parmesan.

WATERMELON AGUACHILE WITH PAPAYA

INGREDIENTS

- 10 dried chiltepín chiles
- Pinch of sugar
- Pinch of kosher salt
- ¼ cup (60 ml) fresh lime juice (from 2 limes)
- ¼ cup (60 ml) fresh orange juice
- 1 pound (455 g) peeled yellow or red watermelon, sliced into ½-inch (1-cm)-thick pieces
- ½ pound (225 g) peeled papaya, seeded and sliced into ½-inch (1-cm)-pieces
- ¾ cup (86 g) thinly sliced red onion
- ½ cup (60 g) thinly sliced cucumber
- ½ cup (58 g) thinly sliced radishes
- A few pinches of flaky sea salt

SERVES 4

Aguachile, which translates to chile water, is a type of ceviche that is made in coastal regions of Mexico. Like a traditional ceviche the seafood is in a way cooked in lime juice, but the lime juice mixture in this case has lots and lots of spicy chilies.

Although aguachile typically is made with shrimp, I made this version with juicy watermelon and buttery papaya, two fruits that along with crunchy cucumber, radish, and red onion do an excellent job of soaking up the spicy citrus marinade.

Let this dish sit for fifteen minutes before diving in. It will give the chile time to be "cooled off" by the sweetness of the fruit and other flavors.

❁ INSTRUCTIONS ❁

In a molcajete (page 29), combine the chiltepín chiles, sugar, and salt. Crush until the chile is in very small pieces, a bit smaller than red chile flakes. Add the lime and orange juice to the molcajete. Stir until combined and all of the chile is unstuck from the sides of the molcajete. If you don't have a molcajete, chop the chiltepín with a sharp knife on a cutting board until it is in very small pieces, then combine with the sugar, salt, and juices in a small bowl.

Arrange the watermelon, papaya, red onion, cucumber, and radishes on a large platter. Pour the chile mixture over the platter and let sit 15 minutes before serving.

WATERMELON RADISH AND HEART OF PALM CEVICHE AVOCADO TOAST

INGREDIENTS

- ½ medium red onion, thinly sliced
- 2 tablespoons (28 ml) fresh lime juice (from 1 lime)
- ½ teaspoon kosher salt, plus more to taste
- 1 can (14 ounces, or 397 g) sliced hearts of palm, drained, rinsed, and cut in half
- 1 cup (116 g) thinly sliced watermelon radishes, cut in half (about 2 small)
- 1 large jalapeño, stemmed and seeded if you'd like it less spicy, and minced
- ¼ cup (4 g) chopped fresh cilantro (tender leaves and stems)
- 3 tablespoons (45 ml) olive oil
- 2 tablespoons (12 g) chopped fresh mint
- 1 tablespoon (4 g) chopped fresh tarragon
- 4 thick slices good seeded bread
- 2 medium ripe avocados, pitted
- A few pinches of ground black pepper

SERVES 4

Avocado toast was like the PB&J of my husband's childhood, so when it exploded in popularity, he was always confused by its newfound fame. The reason it was a popular snack his grandmother used to make him as a boy—and seemingly everyone makes now—is because there's really nothing better.

Crunchy toast, creamy avocado, a sprinkling of salt, it's better for you than jam and more satisfying than plain butter. Avocado reigns supreme when it comes to toast toppings.

We are upping the ante even further by topping our avo toast with a rejuvenating vegan ceviche made with hearts of palm and gorgeous watermelon radish. Enjoy this ceviche on its own or as a crispy tostada, but piled on top of avocado toast makes it more of a substantial lunch or dinner or, heck, breakfast.

❄ INSTRUCTIONS ❄

Place the onion slices in a medium bowl. Toss with the lime juice and salt, and set it aside for 10 minutes.

Add the hearts of palm, radishes, jalapeño, cilantro, oil, mint, and tarragon. Toss well to combine. Let sit at least 15 minutes on the counter or up to 1 hour in the fridge to let the flavors meld together.

Toast the bread slices to your liking; I like just shy of burnt. Slice or scoop an avocado half onto each piece. Mash and spread with a fork if you'd like, and season with salt and black pepper. Spoon the ceviche on top, leaving most of the juice behind.

POWER-UP YOUR VEGGIES

••

Watermelon radishes don't actually taste like watermelons (unfortunately) but they visually bear a resemblance with a green hue that fades to a fuchsia interior. High in vitamin C, potassium, and phosphate, these radishes (which are a variety of daikon radish) are great for digestion and boost immunity. They are best eaten raw in thin slices with a sprinkle of salt. If they are very fresh, you won't have to peel the outer white skin, but if you find it too tough, peel first. If you can't find watermelon radish for this recipe, any thin-sliced radish will work great!

MARINATED VEGETABLE TORTA WITH SERRANO-LIME AIOLI

INGREDIENTS

FOR THE AIOLI

- ½ cup (115 g) mayonnaise
- 1 clove garlic, minced
- 1 serrano chile, stemmed and minced
- 1 teaspoon lime zest

FOR THE MARINATED VEGETABLES

- 2 tablespoons (28 ml) fresh lime juice (from 1 lime)
- 2 tablespoons (30 ml) olive oil
- 2 cloves garlic, minced
- 1 teaspoon orange zest
- 1 teaspoon kosher salt
- ½ teaspoon ground cumin
- 4 large radishes, trimmed and sliced
- 1 small sweet onion, thinly sliced
- 1 can (14 ounces, or 397 g) whole artichoke hearts, drained and each heart cut in half
- 1 large English cucumber, sliced
- 1 large carrot, peeled and thinly sliced
- 1 large, ripe avocado, peeled, pitted, and thinly sliced
- 2 cups (72 g) microgreens or sprouts

FOR THE TORTA

- 4 telera rolls

SERVES 4

●●●●●●●●●●●●●●●●

In the United States, tacos get all the glory, but in Mexico, the torta is loved just as much. A Mexican torta is typically spread with refried beans and avocado, and filled with several shredded meats and cheeses, all stacked incredibly high on soft telera or bolillo rolls.

This veggie-heavy version takes a nutritious turn with tons of crunchy radishes, cucumbers, and carrots quickly marinated in an orange-cumin dressing and piled high on rolls spread with a zesty aioli. Look for Mexican telera rolls at your local Latin market or panadería. The wide, large rolls with a crisp crust and soft interior are the perfect platform for soaking up the flavorful marinade.

❈ INSTRUCTIONS ❈

To make the aioli: Combine all the ingredients in a medium bowl. Stir until evenly mixed. Cover and refrigerate until you are ready to make the tortas.

To make the marinated vegetables: Combine the marinade by mixing the lime juice, oil, garlic, orange zest, salt, and cumin in a large bowl. Add the radishes, onion, artichoke hearts, cucumber, and carrot. Gently toss in the marinade until well coated. Let sit 15 minutes.

Split the rolls in half and spread the aioli on each half. Divide the avocado between the bottom half of each roll. Divide the marinated vegetables among the 4 rolls. Top each with microgreens or sprouts and the top half of the rolls. Slice in half and serve.

CHICKPEA, ROASTED BEET, AND ESCAROLE SALAD WITH SMOKY GOAT CHEESE DRESSING

INGREDIENTS

- 2 cloves garlic, minced
- 6 tablespoons (88 ml) fresh lemon juice (from 3 lemons)
- 2 tablespoons (28 ml) balsamic vinegar
- 2 tablespoons (28 ml) fresh lime juice (from 1 lime)
- 1 tablespoon (20 g) honey
- 1 teaspoon smoked paprika
- 1 teaspoon kosher salt, plus more to taste
- ¼ teaspoon ground black pepper, plus more to taste
- ¼ cup (59 ml) extra-virgin olive oil
- 1 cup (150 g) crumbled chèvre goat cheese
- 1 large head escarole, torn into large pieces
- 1 can (15 ounces, or 425 g) chickpeas, drained and rinsed
- 1 cup (170 g) sliced roasted beets (red or golden or both)
- 1 cup (115 g) Pickled Red Onions (page 126)
- 1 cup (60 g) fresh Italian parsley leaves
- ½ cup (58 g) chopped roasted, salted hazelnuts

SERVES 4

I spent the first decade of my culinary career as a chef working in restaurants from Napa Valley to New York to San Francisco and beyond. No matter where I worked there was always a roasted beet and goat cheese salad on the menu.

I do adore the combination, but I always wanted something more than the typical beets + goat cheese + greens. This is my ideal, and I'd argue the most perfect beet goat cheese salad you'll ever make.

First, it has the spunky punch of pickled red onions, which adds the perfect bite, and instead of delicate mixed greens, this salad's base is buttery escarole, which stands up much nicer to the dense, seriousness of the beets. Then there's the heaping handful of chickpeas, the crunch of roasted hazelnuts, the parsley leaves that act more like a lettuce green than an herb . . . well, I could go on and on, but all you need to do is make it and see.

❊ INSTRUCTIONS ❊

Combine the garlic, lemon juice, balsamic, lime juice, honey, paprika, salt, and black pepper in a medium bowl. Slowly whisk in the oil in a thin stream until incorporated. Gently fold in the goat cheese. Be careful not to break it up too much; you want to keep it in largish hunks.

Arrange the escarole, chickpeas, beets, onions, parsley, and hazelnuts on a large serving platter. Spoon about one-half to three-quarters of the dressing over the top. Sprinkle with salt and pepper, and serve with the remaining dressing on the side.

POWER-UP YOUR VEGGIES

In addition to being low-calorie, beets are also loaded with nutrients that benefit the heart, digestion, and athletic performance. In Tom Robbins's cult classic novel, *Jitterbug Perfume*, beets were the secret to eternal life. I'm not making those promises, but I do believe in their delicious earthy flavor. For this salad you can use store-bought roasted beets or simply roast your own by cooking the beets whole, drizzled with a little olive oil, salt, and pepper, and placed in a covered dish in a 400°F (200°C, or gas mark 6) oven for 40 to 50 minutes, or until easily pierced with a paring knife. Let cool, then peel and slice or dice.

THE BEST EVER MEXICAN TOMATO SANDWICH

INGREDIENTS

- 2 tablespoons (28 g) mayonnaise
- ¾ teaspoon Tajín
- 1 slice of your favorite seeded bread
- 4 fat slices of the best heirloom tomato you can find (ideally freshly picked from your garden)
- Sal de gusano or flaky sea salt

SERVES 1

●●●●●●●●●●●●●●●●●●●

The idea for this sandwich is dead simple. It is an open-faced sandwich—which in my opinion provides the perfect ratio of bread to tomato—meant as an edible love note you give yourself at the height of summer. When tomatoes are at their peak, they need only some crusty bread, creamy mayo, and a touch of salt to shine.

You'll notice this recipe makes just one sandwich. I did this on purpose. I want you to make this when you are by yourself and have a rare moment of peace to embrace the beauty of a perfect tomato sandwich. I suppose you can make more than one at a time and share, but it won't be the same experience.

❀ INSTRUCTIONS ❀

Mix the mayonnaise and Tajín in a small bowl. Taste and add more Tajín if you'd like more spice.

Toast the bread in a toaster to your liking—I'm more of a burnt-toast kinda gal. While the bread is still warm, evenly spread with the mayo. Top the bread with the tomato slices, so they cover as much surface area of the bread as possible. Sprinkle with the sal de gusano. Eat immediately and repeat if needed.

POWER-UP YOUR VEGGIES

●●●●●●●●●●●●●●●●●●●●●●●●●●●●●●●●●●●●●

You want to make this sandwich with only the ripest, most flavorful tomatoes. If you find yourself with tomatoes that are hard, slightly green, or mealy, you'll have to work at them before making the sandwich. I recommend chopping them, sprinkling with salt and a bit of sugar, and roasting them in a 425°F (220°C, or gas mark 7) oven until caramelized and soft. Spoon these roasted tomatoes on the toast and enjoy!

3
FROM THE STOVE

WHAT WOULD I DO WITHOUT MY STOVE AND THE RUSTIC CAST-IRON COMAL THAT SITS ON TOP? THAT CLICK, CLICK, CLICK, THEN WOOSH AS THE FLAME IGNITES, FRIES OUR EGGS IN THE MORNING, REHEATS RICE AND BEANS FOR LUNCH, AND SIMMERS OUR SOUP IN THE EVENING, WARMING EVERY TORTILLA IN BETWEEN.

When cooking vegetables, the stove makes quick work of blanching, boiling, simmering, and sautéing, all techniques that bring out their color, texture, and flavor. Plus, that uniquely Mexican cooking technique—charring.

Sure, you can get that blackened, blistering coat on vegetables over a very hot grill or under the broiler, but neither of those is as easy or effective as heating a comal or cast-iron skillet until it's super hot and searing the onions, tomatoes, and garlic until they are crackling black on the outside and lightly steamed on the inside in minutes.

The stove and comal combination is also essential for warming tortillas, another staple of Mexican cuisine we can't and won't live without. Tortillas (whether corn or flour) must be toasted a bit before eating or cooking with them. For some time now, American cooks have been told they can stack them up in a pile, wrap them in foil or, God forbid, plastic wrap, and heat them in a hot oven or microwave. This results in tortillas that are warm, that is true, but also steamed, wet, sticky, and heartbreakingly sad. A proper tortilla must hit a hot, dry comal to form that irresistible thinnest of crusts, the heat of the pan penetrating through the tortilla, making it pliable and soft.

The recipes in this chapter use the stove top to the fullest, showing off a range of Mexican flavors to suit every appetite: plump sopes (page 65), a cozy soup with corn masa dumplings (page 85), tacos filled with crispy cheese chicharrones (page 90), and even a creamy pasta (page 63). Filling, nutritious dishes the whole family will love.

CREAMY MEXICAN STREET CORN LINGUINE WITH DURITO CRUMBLE

INGREDIENTS

- 1 pound (455 g) linguine
- 2 tablespoons (30 ml) olive oil
- 2 ears sweet corn, kernels removed (or 2 cups [328 g] frozen)
- 1 cup (100 g) thinly sliced scallions, about 3–4 scallions
- 4 cloves garlic, minced
- ½ teaspoon salt, plus more for seasoning
- 1 cup (235 ml) heavy cream
- ½ cup (115 g) Mexican crema (page 23)
- ½ teaspoon chipotle chile powder
- 1 cup (16 g) chopped fresh cilantro (tender leaves and stems)
- ¾ cup (75 g) grated Cotija, divided
- 1 cup (60 g) crushed Mexican duritos (page 27)

SERVES 4

One of the most universally loved Mexican dishes is street corn. When you order it from the cart in Mexico you have two options: elotes or esquites. An elote is essentially grilled corn on the cob, usually with a wooden stick in one end for a handle and coated in crema (or mayonnaise), chile powder, lime, and snowy drifts of grated Cotija cheese. Esquites are just the kernels cut off the cob and served in a cup with a rich, musty corn broth fortified with crema, lime, chile, and cheese.

This soulful pasta dish embraces all the flavors of Mexican street corn and is finished with another beloved street snack: duritos, puffed wheat crisps that make the perfect crispy finish to this indulgent plate of linguine.

❋ INSTRUCTIONS ❋

Cook the linguine in a large pot of heavily salted boiling water until al dente. Drain, reserving ½ cup (120 ml) of the pasta water.

In a large saucepan, heat the oil for 1 to 2 minutes over medium-high heat. Add the corn, scallions, garlic, and salt. Cook for about 5 minutes, stirring occasionally, until the vegetables are tender, fragrant, and vibrant, but not browned.

Add the heavy cream, crema, and chipotle. Bring to a boil, then reduce the heat so the sauce is just simmering. Let simmer until slightly thickened, about 5 minutes.

Return the drained pasta to the large pot it was cooked in and add the sauce, reserved pasta water, cilantro, and ½ cup (50 g) of Cotija. Season with salt and stir well with tongs to coat the linguine evenly.

Divide between bowls. Top each bowl with a large handful of crushed duritos and a sprinkling of the remaining Cotija.

SPINACH, JAMAICA, AND CARAMELIZED ONION SOPES WITH AVOCADO CREMA

INGREDIENTS

FOR THE FILLING

- 4 cups (940 ml) water
- ½ cup (20 g) jamaica (dried hibiscus flowers, page 27), rinsed
- ¼ cup (44 g) chopped pitted prunes
- 1 tablespoon (15 ml) olive oil
- ½ large white onion, sliced
- A few pinches of kosher salt and black pepper
- 1 clove garlic, chopped
- 1 (3-ounce, or 85-g) bunch spinach, tough stems removed
- ½ cup (66 g) crumbled queso fresco (optional)

FOR THE AVOCADO CREMA

- 1 large, ripe avocado, peeled and pitted
- ¼ cup (60 ml) water
- 2 tablespoons (28 ml) fresh lime juice (from 1 lime)
- 2 tablespoons (30 ml) avocado oil
- 1 cup (16 g) fresh cilantro (tender leaves and stems)
- 1 teaspoon kosher salt
- 1 teaspoon lime zest
- ¼ teaspoon arbol chile powder (optional)

FOR THE SOPES

- 1 cup (29 g) masa harina
- ½ teaspoon kosher salt
- 1–1½ cups (235–355 ml) boiling water

SERVES 4 TO 6

S opes are just one of the hundreds of things you can make with a lemon-sized ball of masa dough. This simple combination of masa harina, water, and salt can be shaped, filled, flattened, toasted, fried, or baked into a mind-blowing array of snacks, sides, and meals.

If you are lucky enough to find fresh masa, which is simply rehydrated field corn that has been ground into a dough, I encourage you to play around with that as well. You can use it just as it is, no need to add anything. Form it into the sopes shape described below and cook as instructed.

The sopes are best made and eaten right away. If you'd like to make them in advance, keep them warm in a clean kitchen towel or tortilla warmer. Then rewarm when you are ready to eat by brushing the bottoms with a little oil, filling them with the jamaica mixture, and toasting in a hot frying pan, covered with the lid, until hot to the touch.

You can adjust the size of the sopes to make them into one- or two-bite appetizers by simply using less masa dough (about a walnut-sized piece) or larger dinner-sized sopes by using a bigger, lemon-sized ball of dough.

❀ INSTRUCTIONS ❀

To prepare the jamaica: Combine the water and flowers in a large saucepan over medium-high heat. Bring to a boil and cook for 10 minutes. Remove from the heat, add the prunes, and let steep until very soft, about 2 hours.

Once very tender, set a fine-mesh sieve over a large container. Drain the jamaica and reserve the cooking liquid to make Agua de Jamaica (page 181). Set the mixture aside.

Meanwhile, to make the avocado crema: Combine all the ingredients in a blender and blend until very smooth. Taste and add more salt or lime juice, if needed. Cover and refrigerate until ready to serve.

To make the sopes: Combine the masa harina and salt in a large bowl. Add the water, starting with 1 cup (235 ml), and mix with a wooden spoon. Add more water a bit at a time, until a soft, supple dough forms. Cover with plastic wrap, and set aside while you make the filling.

Continued >

Heat the oil a large frying pan over medium heat. Once shimmering, add the onion and season with salt and pepper. Cook, stirring occasionally, until golden brown and soft, about 10 to 15 minutes. Add the jamaica-prune mixture, garlic, and spinach. Cook, stirring until the spinach is just wilted. Taste and add more salt, if needed. Cover and keep warm while you cook the sopes.

Heat a comal or cast-iron skillet over medium heat for at least 3 minutes, or until hot but not smoking. While the comal is heating, grab a lemon-sized piece of dough, and roll into a smooth ball. If the ball cracks while you roll it, return the piece you just grabbed to the bowl, add more hot water to the dough, a tablespoon at a time, and work in until it is soft. If it sticks badly to your hands, flour your hands with masa harina, then start again.

Pat the ball between your palms, back and forth, until it is a ½-inch (1-cm)-thick round. Place the round on the hot comal and let cook, undisturbed, until a crust forms and easily moves around in the pan, about 3 minutes. Flip and cook for an additional 3 minutes, or until they feel firm and not squishy when you press on them.

Remove the sope from the pan and let cool for 1 minute or so, just long enough to keep your hands from burning. Make a slightly raised border around the sope by pinching the edge between your thumb and index finger to create a retaining wall of sorts. Repeat with the remaining dough.

Spoon a dollop of avocado crema on top of the warm sopes, then a spoonful of filling and some crumbled queso fresco (if using). Any leftover filling makes excellent tacos or quesadillas.

BEAN AND RAJAS VOLTEADAS WITH CHIPOTLE-PILONCILLO SALSA

INGREDIENTS

FOR THE CHIPOTLE-PILONCILLO SALSA

- 5 dried chipotle chiles, stems and seeds removed, and rinsed
- 2½ cups (570 ml) water
- ¼ medium white onion
- 1 cone (1 ounce, or 28 g) piloncillo (page 27)
- 1 clove garlic
- ½ teaspoon kosher salt

FOR THE RAJAS

- 1 large poblano pepper

FOR THE VOLTEADAS

- 4 (8- to 10-inch, or 20- to 25-cm) flour tortillas
- 4 cups (400 g) shredded mozzarella cheese
- 1⅓ cups (360 g) Refried Beans (page 99), warm

SERVES 4

The word *voltear* means to flip or turn around, and that's exactly what happens with these inside out quesadillas. This dish is extra special because both the volteadas and the salsa are recipes I've learned from two dear friends and excellent Mexican cooks. The volteadas are a trick I picked up from my friend, Karla Zazueta, who makes these crispy, cheese-lined quesadillas for her kids, who just adore them. The sweet-and-spicy chipotle salsa was inspired from friend and vegan food blogger Alejandra Graf, who is a constant source of plant-based inspiration. Serve with Cilantro-Lime Slaw (page 179) to round out the meal.

❋ INSTRUCTIONS ❋

To make the chipotle-piloncillo salsa: Combine all the ingredients in a small saucepan. Bring to a boil over medium-high heat. Reduce the heat to a simmer and cook, stirring occasionally, until the piloncillo has completely dissolved and the chiles are soft, about 20 minutes. Remove from the heat, let cool slightly, then pour into a blender and blend until smooth.

To make the rajas: Place the poblano pepper over a gas flame on the stove. If you don't have a gas range, you can also do this under a broiler or on a grill. Roast until the skin is charred on all sides, about 5 minutes. Place in a heatproof bowl and cover with plastic wrap until cool enough to handle, about 5 to 10 minutes. Rub the blackened skin off the pepper with your fingers. Then remove the stem and seeds, and rinse under cold water. Pat dry and slice into thin strips.

To make the volteadas: Heat a cast-iron or nonstick frying pan over medium heat. When hot, but not smoking, add a tortilla to the pan and spread 1 cup (100 g) of the cheese in a thin layer over the tortilla. Toast the tortilla until the cheese just starts to melt. Flip so the cheese is directly hitting the pan and cook until golden brown, but not burnt, about 1 to 2 minutes.

Use a metal spatula to flip back over onto a plate, top one half of the tortilla with a quarter of the rajas and a quarter of the beans, and fold the other side over to cover. Repeat with the remaining tortillas, cheese, and fillings. Serve immediately with the salsa.

WINTER VEGETABLE ENMOLADAS WITH QUESO FRESCO

INGREDIENTS

- 2 large carrots, peeled and diced
- 1 medium rutabaga or large russet potato, peeled and diced
- ½ large head Romesco broccoli or broccoli florets, trimmed and diced
- 1 tablespoon (14 g) softened butter
- A few pinches of kosher salt
- 2 cups Instant Pot Mole Amarillo (page 100) or ½ cup (120 g) store-bought mole paste mixed with 2 cups (475 ml) vegetable broth
- 12–18 (6-inch, or 15-cm) corn tortillas
- 1 cup (132 g) crumbled queso fresco
- ¼ cup (32 g) minced red onion

SERVES 4 TO 6

I'm sure you've heard of enchiladas, but do you know where the name comes from? *Enchilar* means to smother something in chile sauce (it also means to annoy someone, which makes total sense). In that vein, if enchiladas mean tortillas covered in chile sauce, then *enmoladas* mean tortillas covered in mole sauce.

These enmoladas more resemble crepes than the rolled, baked, and smothered in cheese enchiladas you know and love. (I love them too and there's a recipe for them on page 153). The glossy mole is the real star here; the tortillas are the vehicle, and the veggies are just a nice textural contrast. Use the Mole Amarillo recipe (page 100) or rehydrate store-bought mole paste with some vegetable broth.

❀ INSTRUCTIONS ❀

Bring a large saucepan of heavily salted water to a boil. Add the carrots and rutabaga. Cook until just tender, but not soft—there should still be some bite in the middle—about 3 to 4 minutes. Remove to a medium bowl with a slotted spoon or a bamboo skimmer. Add the broccoli and cook until just tender, about 2 to 3 minutes. Remove the broccoli to the bowl with the carrot and rutabaga. Add the butter to the bowl. Toss until the butter is melted and the vegetables are coated. Taste and season with salt, if needed. Cover and keep warm.

Heat the mole sauce in a large, deep frying pan until barely simmering. Heat a comal or cast-iron skillet over medium heat for at least 3 minutes, or until hot but not smoking. Warm the tortillas on the comal, then transfer to the mole sauce, flipping to coat both sides in the sauce. Using tongs, gently fold the tortilla in half, trapping some of the mole sauce inside the fold. Transfer to a serving platter. Top with the vegetables, cheese, and red onion. Serve immediately.

Continued >

SQUASH BLOSSOM QUESADILLAS WITH TOMATILLO-AVOCADO SALSA

INGREDIENTS

FOR THE SALSA

- 1 pound (455 g) tomatillos, husks removed, rinsed, and cut in half
- 1½–2 cups (24–32 g) chopped fresh cilantro (tender leaves and stems)
- 1 medium jalapeño, stemmed and cut into 2–3 pieces
- 1 medium ripe avocado, peeled and pitted
- ½ small white onion, cut into 2–3 pieces
- 1½–2 teaspoons kosher salt, plus more to taste

Every time I make squash blossoms, I am surprised all over again by how much I love them. The edible flowers of squash plants are very common in Mexican cooking, especially in the southern region of Oaxaca, where these quesadillas stuffed with stringy cheese and the sunshine yellow blossoms are as familiar as our PB&Js here.

If you've never worked with Oaxaca cheese, getting it to shred properly takes some practice. It is similar to mozzarella cheese and the motion is that of pulling strings from a mozzarella cheese stick. Oaxaca cheese pros can take a piece and turn it into a heaping pile of gossamer strands. If you can get it into even ¼-inch (6-mm)-thick pieces, that's great. You can also cheat and use a cheese grater.

Continued

FOR THE QUESADILLAS

- 2 tablespoons (30 ml) avocado or sunflower oil
- 1 medium white onion, thinly sliced
- A few pinches of kosher salt and black pepper
- 4 cloves garlic, sliced
- 2 bunches squash blossoms, stems and stamens removed and thickly sliced or torn into large pieces (about 4 cups [220 g] sliced squash blossoms)
- 4 large (8- to 10-inch, or 20- to 25-cm) flour tortillas
- 12 ounces (340 g) queso Oaxaca, shredded

SERVES 4

❈ INSTRUCTIONS ❈

To make the salsa: Add all the ingredients to a blender. Blend on high until very smooth. Dip a spoon in the salsa. It should easily run off the spoon with just a thin veil of salsa remaining on the back of the spoon and not be gloppy. Add water, ¼ cup (60 ml) at a time until this consistency is achieved. Dip a chip, tostada, or cracker in; taste and add more salt, if needed. Transfer to a mason jar, cover, and refrigerate until ready to serve. The salsa can be made up to 3 days in advance.

To make the quesadillas: Heat the oil in a large frying pan over medium-high heat. Add the onion, and season with salt and black pepper. Sauté, stirring occasionally, until light brown. Add the garlic for the last minute of cooking, just to get it a little tender, then add the squash blossoms. Sauté for 1 minute, until wilted, and remove from the heat.

Heat a comal or cast-iron skillet over medium heat for at least 3 minutes, or until hot but not smoking. Place 1 to 2 flour tortillas (don't overlap) on the comal to warm one side. Flip and add one-quarter of the filling and cheese onto one half of each tortilla. Fold the other half down to cover and cook for about 3 minutes, or until the cheese begins to melt and the tortilla is golden and toasted. Flip and cook until toasted on the other side, about 2 to 3 minutes.

Remove and let cool for 1 to 2 minutes; otherwise the cheese will gush out. Cut into quarters or in half, and serve with the salsa.

POTATO AND COLLARD GREEN CRISPY TACOS WITH ANCHO CHILE CREMA

INGREDIENTS

FOR THE CHILE CREMA

- ½ cup (115 g) Mexican crema (page 23)
- 2 tablespoons (28 ml) fresh lime juice (from 1 lime)
- 2 teaspoons (4 g) ground ancho chile powder
- 1 teaspoon lime zest
- ½ teaspoon kosher salt

FOR THE TACOS

- 1 pound (455 g) Yukon gold potatoes, peeled and quartered (about 4 small)
- 1 clove garlic, peeled
- 1 tablespoon (15 g) plus 1 teaspoon (5 g) kosher salt, divided
- 1 bunch collard greens, stems removed and chopped
- ½ teaspoon ground white pepper
- 12 (6-inch, or 15-cm) corn tortillas
- ½ cup (118 ml) avocado or sunflower oil

SERVES 4 TO 6

These crunchy, hard-shell tacos go by many names: tacos dorados, basket tacos, or tacos de papa. All refer to the same thing, a sturdy corn tortilla stuffed with soft, fluffy potatoes, and lightly fried so the outside is shatteringly crisp. One bite reveals pockets of fluffy potatoes and silky bits of collard greens.

❊ INSTRUCTIONS ❊

To make the ancho chile crema: Combine all the ingredients in a medium bowl. Whisk until smooth, and set aside.

To make the tacos: Place the potatoes and garlic in a large saucepan. Fill with water, add a generous tablespoon of salt, and bring to a boil.

Add the collard greens and gently boil until the potatoes can be easily pierced with a knife, about 20 to 25 minutes. Drain well, return to the pan, and add the white pepper. Mash with a potato masher, until mostly smooth with a few pieces of potato here and there. Taste and add salt, if needed.

Heat a comal or cast-iron skillet over medium heat for at least 3 minutes, or until hot but not smoking. Warm the tortillas one or two at a time (don't overlap) until hot to the touch and flexible, but not toasted. Keep warm in a tortilla warmer or wrapped in a clean kitchen towel.

Heat the oil in a large, deep frying pan over medium-high heat.

While the oil is heating, place about ¼ cup (70 g) of potato filling on one side of each tortilla. Fold the other side of the tortilla over the filling and pinch the edges together to seal. They won't seal all the way, but the potato filling will keep them together in the oil.

Dip one side of one taco in the oil to see if it is hot enough. The oil should bubble up over the taco as soon as you dip it in. If it doesn't, give it another minute to heat up and try again.

Fry 2 to 3 tacos at a time (don't overlap) in the hot oil until golden brown and crisp on both sides, about 2 minutes per side. Drain on paper towels, sprinkle with salt, and serve with the crema.

Continued ›

POWER-UP YOUR VEGGIES

Like many dark, leafy greens, collard greens are a nutritional powerhouse. Packed with bone-fortifying vitamins and minerals, they are fantastic food for people sticking to a plant-based diet. Don't be thrown off by their reputation for having to be cooked to death. They take no more effort than kale, chard, or any other green. Simply remove the tough stem by slicing on either side with a sharp knife and eat raw, steamed, sautéed, or, in the case of this recipe, boiled.

VEGAN PICADILLO TOSTADAS WITH RICE AND PEAS

Whenever we visit my mother-in-law, the kids always request two things: red rice and picadillo. She uses ground beef, as is traditional, but I wanted to see if I could make something similar using a plant-based meat substitute. The first time I made this for dinner, not a single soul could tell the difference. It's that good.

You can find fried tostadas at your local grocery store, but I hardly ever buy them because toasting them in the oven is so much better for you and they have a fantastic crunch. If you'd like to try your hand at frying them, turn to page 145. If you'd prefer to use store-bought ones instead, though, go for it!

Continued >

INGREDIENTS

FOR THE TOSTADAS

- 12 (6-inch, or 15-cm) corn tortillas

FOR THE PICADILLO

- 2 tablespoons (30 ml) avocado or sunflower oil
- 1 medium white onion, chopped
- 2 medium carrots, chopped
- 3 cloves garlic, chopped
- 3 small Yukon gold potatoes, peeled and diced (about 9 ounces [255 g])
- 1 pound (455 g) plant-based beef
- 1 recipe (10 g) Magic Spice Mix! (page 19)
- 1¼ cups (295 ml) Mexican Pilsner-style beer (such as Victoria) or water
- ½ cup (65 g) frozen peas (no need to thaw)
- ¼ cup (15 g) chopped fresh Italian parsley

FOR SERVING

- 3 cups (474 g) steamed rice or Oven-Baked Garlic-Cilantro Rice (page 175)
- Lime wedges from a couple limes
- 1 large, ripe avocado, diced
- 1–2 medium jalapeños, thinly sliced
- 1 recipe tomatillo-avocado salsa (page 73)

SERVES 4 TO 6

❋ INSTRUCTIONS ❋

To make the tostadas: Preheat the oven to 350°F (175°C, or gas mark 4). Once the oven is ready, lay the tortillas directly on the oven racks with plenty of room around them for air to circulate. (I put six on the top rack and six on the bottom in my oven.) Bake for about 15 minutes, turning the tortillas halfway through, until they are very crisp and crack if you break them. Look for a light brown color, no darker than the shade of a roasted peanut. Remove the tortillas to a serving platter.

To make the picadillo: Heat the oil in a large frying pan over medium-high heat. Add the onion, carrots, garlic, and potatoes. Cook until the garlic and onions start to brown, about 5 minutes.

Add the plant-based beef and spice mix, breaking up the meat with the back of a wooden spoon. Continue cooking until the beef is browned, about 3 minutes. Add the beer, reduce the heat to medium-low, and cover. Simmer the picadillo for about 10 minutes, or until the veggies are tender. Stir in the peas and parsley, and cook for about 1 minute.

To serve: Spread ¼ cup (about 40 g) of rice on a tostada, and top with ¼ cup (60 ml) picadillo. Pass the garnishes at the table.

POWER-UP YOUR VEGGIES

There are many plant-based meats available and most will cook up remarkably similar to ground beef. They are protein-rich and full of fiber, calcium, and potassium with zero cholesterol. Plus, producing these "meats" is much easier on the planet. Try a few different brands before settling on your favorite as they all are unique.

POACHED EGGS DIVORCIADOS

This may seem like a complicated dish to pull off for breakfast—I mean who has time to whip up two salsas before 9 a.m.? But broken up into parts makes it a quick meal. The salsas can be made three or four days in advance, so if you do like I do, and keep your fridge stocked with at least two types of salsa all the time, you can have huevos divorciados (or divorced eggs) whenever the urge hits!

Continued >

INGREDIENTS

FOR THE CHARRED TOMATO SALSA

- 2 large, ripe tomatoes, cored
- ½ medium white onion, cut in half
- 2 medium jalapeños, stems removed
- ½ cup (8 g) fresh cilantro (tender leaves and stems)
- ½ cup (120 ml) water
- 1 teaspoon kosher salt, plus more to taste

FOR THE SALSA VERDE

- 2 pounds (907 g) tomatillos, husks removed and rinsed
- 1 small white onion, quartered
- 2 cloves garlic
- 2 medium jalapeños, stems removed
- 1–2 teaspoons salt
- ¾ cup (12 g) fresh cilantro (tender leaves and stems)

FOR THE POACHED EGGS

- 8 eggs
- 1 teaspoon distilled white vinegar

SERVES 4

● ● ● ● ● ● ● ● ● ● ● ● ● ● ● ● ●

❅ INSTRUCTIONS ❅

To make the charred tomato salsa: Heat a comal or cast-iron skillet over medium heat for at least 3 minutes, or until hot but not smoking. Place the tomatoes, onion, and jalapeños on the hot comal and let cook, undisturbed, until charred and blackened. Turn and continue cooking until charred on all sides. Some vegetables may char quicker than others. Remove them as they are ready. This should take about 30 minutes total.

Transfer the charred vegetables to a blender. Add the cilantro, water, and salt. Start blending on low and gradually increase the speed to high, until smooth and completely pureed. Dip a spoon in the salsa. It should easily run off the spoon with just a thin veil of salsa remaining on the back of the spoon and not be gloppy at all. Add water, ¼ cup (60 ml) at a time, until this consistency is achieved.

Dip a chip, tostada, or cracker in; taste and add more salt, if needed. Transfer to a mason jar, cover, and refrigerate until ready to serve. The salsa can be made up to 3 days in advance.

To make the salsa verde: Combine the tomatillos, onion, garlic, jalapeños, and 1 teaspoon of salt in a small saucepan. Cover with water, bring to a boil, then reduce the heat to a simmer. Cook until the tomatillos are just tender, have changed color from bright green to a more grayish green, but have not burst open, about 10 minutes.

Using a slotted spoon, transfer the vegetables to a blender. Add ½ cup (120 ml) of the cooking liquid and the cilantro. Start blending on low and gradually increase the speed to high, until the mixture is smooth. Repeat the same process as you did with the charred tomato salsa to see if the consistency and salt amount are good. Instead of adding straight-up water to this one for the consistency, you'll add the tomatillo cooking liquid. Transfer to a mason jar, cover, and refrigerate until you are ready to serve. The salsa can be made up to 3 days in advance.

When you're ready to serve, pour each salsa into two small saucepans or frying pans and keep warm over medium-low heat.

To make the eggs: Bring about 8 cups (1.9 L) or at least 2 inches (5 cm) of water to a simmer in a large saucepan. Add the vinegar.

Break an egg, one at a time, into a small ramekin. Stir the water in the saucepan in a circle to create a vortex in the middle. Gently, but quickly, add the egg into the middle of the vortex. I think it's easiest to cook the eggs one at a time. Cook until the whites are just set, about 3 minutes.

Remove with a slotted spoon and transfer to a paper towel–lined plate. Dab off any excess water, then move to a plate. Repeat with the other eggs, serving two eggs per plate. Spoon the charred tomato salsa over one egg and the salsa verde over the other egg. Serve immediately with warm corn tortillas.

CHILEATOLE WITH MASA DUMPLINGS AND LIME CREMA

INGREDIENTS

FOR THE LIME CREMA

- ½ cup (115 g) Mexican crema (page 23)
- 1 teaspoon lime zest
- 1 tablespoon (15 ml) lime juice (from 1 lime)

FOR THE CHILEATOLE

- 2 ounces (55 g) dried guajillo chiles, about 4 medium chiles
- 2 dried arbol chiles
- 6 tablespoons (89 ml) avocado or sunflower oil
- 2 medium white onions, chopped
- 3 cloves garlic, chopped
- 1 tablesppon (18 g) kosher salt, plus more to taste
- 1 sprig fresh Mexican oregano
- 8 cups (1.9 L) water
- 1 pound (455 g) Yukon gold potatoes, peeled and cut in half or quartered if large (about 4 small potatoes)
- ½ cup (8 g) chopped fresh cilantro (tender leaves and stems)

FOR THE DUMPLINGS

- 1 cup (116 g) masa harina
- ¾ cup (175 ml) water
- 2 tablespoons (9 g) coconut oil
- 1 teaspoon kosher salt

SERVES 4 TO 6

● ● ● ● ● ● ● ● ● ● ● ● ● ● ●

In the winter, having a warm mug of creamy atole is the Mexican equivalent of a cup of hot cocoa. This sweet cinnamon drink is thickened with masa harina, the same corn flour used to make tortillas and tamales. Chileatole is the same idea of a corn flour–thickened liquid, but instead of a sweet, belly-warming drink, it's a chile-laced soup that will fulfill those same cozy cravings. The base of the soup is dried guajillo chiles, which are herbaceous and earthy, but not spicy. I've also added a couple of arbol chiles for their warming heat, but leave them out if you'd rather keep it mild. The fluffy dumplings that thicken the soup have the most beautiful name: chochoyotes (show-show-yo-tes). These corn flour disks are indented with your thumb right before they hit the pot, making a perfect vessel to trap even more of the rich chile broth.

❈ INSTRUCTIONS ❈

To make the lime crema: Combine all the ingredients in a small bowl. Whisk until smooth. Cover and refrigerate until ready to use.

To make the chileatole: Remove the stems and seeds from the dried chiles, and rinse. Heat a small saucepan of water to a boil, add the chiles, and remove from the heat. Let sit until very soft and tender, about 30 to 40 minutes.

Heat 2 tablespoons (30 ml) of oil in a large, heavy-bottomed Dutch oven or soup pot over medium-high heat. Add the onions and garlic, and season with salt. Cook, stirring occasionally, until starting to brown, about 5 minutes.

Scrape the browned onions and garlic into a blender, and return the pot to the stove. Remove the soaked chiles with tongs and save the soaking liquid. Add the chiles to the blender. Add the leaves from the sprig of oregano and ½ cup (120 ml) of the soaking liquid, and the tablespoon of salt. Blend on high until very smooth.

In the Dutch oven you used to brown the onions, add ¼ cup (59 ml) more oil and heat over medium heat. Once the oil is shimmering, pour the chile mixture into the hot oil, stirring continuously—be careful, the sauce will spatter. Fry the chile mixture for 4 to 5 minutes, or until it changes color from a bright red to a deeper brownish red and is fragrant.

Continued ›

Pour the water into the blender jar and swish it around to get the remaining sauce out. Pour this chile water into the pot along with the potatoes, and bring to a boil. Reduce the heat to a gentle simmer. Cover and cook until the potatoes are tender, about 20 minutes.

Meanwhile, to make the masa dumplings: Combine the masa harina, water, coconut oil, and salt in a large bowl. Mix well with your hands, breaking up any larger pieces of coconut oil into small pea-sized bits. Form into walnut-sized balls (you should have about 16), then flatten slightly and press your thumb in the middle to create an indentation.

Once a paring knife easily slips into the potatoes, add the chochoyotes in a single layer on top of the broth. Let simmer for 5 to 6 minutes, then gently fold the dumplings into the broth being careful not to break them up. Cover the pot and simmer until the dumplings are firm and don't smash when you nudge them with a spoon and the broth has thickened, about 20 minutes. Taste and add more salt, if needed.

Stir the cilantro into the soup, then ladle it into bowls. Top with a dollop of lime crema and serve.

JACKFRUIT TINGA GRAIN BOWL

Mexican chef Enrique Olvera has said tinga is the first recipe every Mexican learns when they leave home because it is basically foolproof and made with very few ingredients. Just a simple sauce of tomatoes, chipotles, onions, and garlic is all you need to make this flavor-packed dinner.

Tinga is typically made with chicken, but I've substituted jackfruit—the wildly affordable, texturally similar, plant-based meat substitute that comes ready to use in a can. This is my dream grain bowl, chewy barley, fresh, crunchy radishes, roasted sweet potato, saucy tinga. You don't have to add all the toppings, but I highly recommend it.

Continued >

INGREDIENTS

FOR THE JACKFRUIT TINGA

- 2 tablespoons (30 ml) avocado or sunflower oil
- 1 large white onion, chopped
- A few pinches of kosher salt
- 3 cloves garlic, chopped
- 3 large tomatoes, chopped
- 3 chipotles in adobo, chopped
- 1 can (20 ounces, or 567 g) green jackfruit in brine, drained and rinsed
- ½ cup (120 ml) water

FOR THE BOWL

- 3 cups (705 ml) water
- 1 cup (200 g) pearled barley
- A few pinches of kosher salt
- 1 large sweet potato
- 2 tablespoons (30 ml) plus 1 teaspoon avocado or sunflower oil
- 1 tablespoon (5 g) Magic Spice Mix! (page 19)
- ½ cup (70 g) raw pumpkin seeds
- 1 large, ripe avocado, peeled, pitted, and diced
- 1 cup (16 g) fresh cilantro leaves, sprouts, or microgreens
- 1 cup (230 g) Mexican crema (page 23) or Avocado Crema (page 65), if you want to keep it vegan
- 4 medium radishes, thinly sliced
- 1 cup (132 g) crumbled queso fresco (optional)

SERVES 4 TO 6

To make the jackfruit tinga: Heat the oil in a large frying pan over medium-high heat. Add the onion and season with salt. Cook, stirring occasionally, until beginning to soften, about 3 minutes. Add the garlic and cook for 1 minute. Stir in the tomatoes and chipotles, and season again with salt. Let cook until the tomatoes have cooked down a bit and formed a sauce.

Take pieces of jackfruit and break them up with your hands as you add them to the pan. Add the ½ cup (120 ml) of water, bring to a boil, then reduce the heat to medium-low. Cook until jackfruit is warmed through, about 5 minutes. Reduce heat to low, cover and keep warm while you prepare the rest of the bowl ingredients.

To prepare the bowl: Make the barley by combining the water, barley, and a pinch of salt and bring to a boil. Reduce the heat to a simmer, cover, and cook until tender, about 25 to 30 minutes.

Preheat the oven to 400°F (200°C, or gas mark 6). Peel and dice the sweet potato. Place it on a sheet pan, drizzle with the 2 tablespoons (30 ml) of oil, and sprinkle with Magic Spice. Toss to coat, then spread in a single layer and roast until tender and golden brown, about 30 minutes.

Heat the teaspoon of oil in a small frying pan over medium heat. Add the pepitas and sprinkle with salt. Cook, stirring constantly, until they turn from grayish green to golden brown and start to pop. Scrape onto a plate to stop the cooking.

To assemble the bowls: Divide the barley between the bowls, then arrange the jackfruit tinga, roasted sweet potatoes, avocado, cilantro, crema, radishes, and queso fresco (if using) on top. Sprinkle the pepitas over everything and serve.

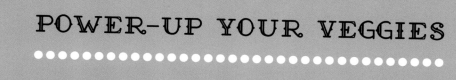

POWER-UP YOUR VEGGIES

• •

Jackfruit is the newest "meat substitute" to hit the scene in the last few years. This staple of many Asian cuisines is the definition of plant power. High in protein, potassium, and vitamin B with only 95 calories per cup, it is nutritionally and texturally an ideal alternative. Many grocery stores sell fresh chunks of this gigantic fruit (some grow to be up to 100 pounds), but the canned green jackfruit in brine is best for this recipe.

CHEESE CHICHARRÓN TACOS WITH CHARRED SCALLIONS AND SPICY GUACAMOLE

Chicharrones typically refers to bubbly, crisp, fried pork skin, but the term is also synonymous with anything with that same immaculate crunch. For these tacos, we fry handfuls of aged Gouda in a hot pan until they turn golden and crisp and crackling. These cheesy treats make addictive tacos, especially when combined with charred scallions and chile-packed guacamole.

INGREDIENTS

FOR THE SPICY GUACAMOLE

- ¼ medium white onion, minced
- 4 serrano chiles, stems removed and minced
- ⅓ cup (6 g) minced fresh cilantro (tender leaves and stems)
- 2 large, ripe avocados, pitted
- ¼ cup (60 ml) fresh lime juice (from 2 limes)
- 1 teaspoon kosher salt

FOR THE CHARRED SCALLIONS

- 1 bunch scallions, ends trimmed
- 1 tablespoon (15 ml) olive oil
- A few pinches of kosher salt and black pepper

FOR THE TACOS

- 6 (4-in, or 10-cm) corn tortillas
- 8 ounces (225 g) aged Gouda, shredded

SERVES 4 TO 6

The one question my husband always asks when I make a batch of any salsa is "Is it spicy?" For him, if it doesn't leave your tongue tingling, it's not salsa. This is the guacamole I make for him, with four fiery serrano chiles. If you don't like things that spicy, lower the amount of chiles or remove the seeds and white ribs that hold the seeds in place (this is where most of the heat lies). To keep it from turning brown, press a piece of plastic wrap directly on top of the surface of the guacamole. Then cover the bowl with another piece of tightly stretched plastic wrap.

❋ INSTRUCTIONS ❋

To make the guacamole: Combine the onion, serranos, and cilantro in a medium bowl. Scoop the avocado flesh out of the skin with a large spoon and place it in the bowl. Mash the mixture with a potato masher. Add the lime juice, sprinkle the salt on top, then mix with a large spoon.

To make the scallions: Heat a grill pan or cast-iron skillet on a grill. Drizzle the scallions with oil, and season with salt and pepper. Place the scallions on the pan and cook, undisturbed, until lightly charred on one side, then turn and continue cooking until charred on all sides, about 10 minutes. Remove to a cutting board, then cut into large pieces.

To make the tacos: Heat a comal or cast-iron skillet over medium heat for at least 3 minutes, or until hot but not smoking. Heat the tortillas on the comal, and keep them warm in a tortilla warmer or clean kitchen towel. Heat a dry,

nonstick frying pan over medium-low heat. When it's hot, but not smoking, sprinkle a heaping ¼ cup (55 g) of cheese into a 3-inch (7.5-cm) circle on a the pan. Let cook, undisturbed, for 3 minutes, or until the cheese has turned from white to golden. Remove the pan from the heat and let cool for 30 seconds to 1 minute to firm slightly. Flip the cheese with an offset spatula or a metal spatula. The cheese will wrinkle when you scoop it, and that's okay. Just flatten it again after you flip it. Return to the heat and cook for about 1 minute, until golden brown underneath. Repeat with the remaining cheese, frying ¼ cup (55 g) at a time.

To assemble the tacos: Fill each tortilla with a cheese chicharrón and a few pieces of charred scallions, and serve with the spicy guacamole.

FIDEO SECO WITH TOMATO SALSA, MEXICAN CREMA, ROASTED KALE, AND QUESO FRESCO

INGREDIENTS

- 1 can (28 ounces, or 794 g) tomatoes
- ¼ cup (59 ml) plus 3 tablespoons (45 ml) olive oil, divided
- 2 cloves garlic
- 1 tablespoon (4 g) chopped fresh Mexican oregano
- 1 teaspoon kosher salt
- 1 bag (7 ounces, or 196 g) fideo pasta
- 1 recipe Chipotle-Garlic Roasted Kale (page 175)
- ½ cup (115 g) Mexican crema (page 23)
- ½ cup (66 g) queso fresco

SERVES 4 TO 6

This simple bowl of comfort is how Mexicans do pasta. Thin vermicelli noodles get toasted in hot oil before being mixed with tomato sauce, giving it an extra layer of flavor. Topped with Mexican crema, roasted kale, and fresh, crumbled cheese turns it into an easy, satisfying meal.

The tomato sauce is the same one I make all the time and use for everything from pizza sauce to a quick tomato soup. It works great as a basic tomato sauce for traditional, Italian-style boiled pasta as well.

❈ INSTRUCTIONS ❈

In a blender, combine the tomatoes, ¼ cup (59 ml) of oil, garlic, oregano, and salt. Blend on high until smooth.

Heat the remaining 3 tablespoons (45 ml) of oil in a large, deep frying pan over medium heat. Add the fideo and toast, stirring frequently, until the pasta is golden brown and has lost its sheen, about 4 minutes.

Stir the tomato sauce into the pan with the fideo. Reduce the heat to low and simmer until the pasta is cooked, about 15 minutes, stirring frequently to prevent sticking. Remove from the heat, cover, and steam, about 5 minutes.

Serve in large bowls with the roasted kale and garnished with the crema and queso fresco.

4
INSTANT POT

I'M NOT BIG ON KITCHEN EQUIPMENT. I'VE NEVER HAD A LARGE KITCHEN AND LEARNED HOW TO COOK IN RESTAURANT KITCHENS WHERE YOUR DESIGNATED WORK SPACE IS AS WIDE AS A TWO-FOOT CUTTING BOARD. IN THESE CRAMPED QUARTERS I'VE RELIED ON A SHARP CHEF'S KNIFE, A GAS RANGE, AND A BLENDER TO GET THINGS DONE.

However, as a busy working mother who is rarely organized enough to have a dinner plan, I loooooove my Instant Pot. Take dried beans for example: a pot of beans (that I never even soaked) is ready in about an hour. Compare that to the overnight soaking, plus three hours of cook time they take on the stove. For a family that eats beans practically every night, that was a HUGE game changer.

And it's so versatile! This section has way more than bean recipes or soup recipes (although it does have both of those things, and I would happily eat them any day of the week). Your Instant Pot can do those things and so much more: Casseroles! Hard-boiled eggs! Sweet potatoes! And all in a fraction of the time. Insane, right?!

A note about which Instant Pot to use: These recipes were made for a 6-quart Instant Pot. Make sure your machine is the same size before beginning. If you own a smaller 3-quart model, cut the recipes in half to make sure they don't exceed the volume of your machine.

SOFRITO BLACK BEANS: THREE WAYS

INGREDIENTS

- 1 pound (455 g) dried black beans
- 2 tablespoons (30 ml) olive oil
- 1 large white onion, chopped
- 3 cloves garlic, chopped
- 2 serrano chiles, stemmed and chopped
- 2½ teaspoons (6 g) ground cumin
- 2 teaspoons (4 g) guajillo chile powder
- 1½ teaspoons ground coriander
- ¾ teaspoon dried epazote (page 14) or dried oregano
- 3 medium tomatoes, cored and chopped
- 5 cups (1.2 L) water
- 1–2 tablespoons (15–30 g) kosher salt

SERVES 6 TO 8

A pot of beans may seem like a simple thing, but it took me a long time to learn how to make them actually taste good. When my husband and I started dating, I would make a pot of beans and he would politely eat them because he loves me but would say things like, "Maybe add more water." Or "More chiles would be nice." I didn't get it; those beans were spicy as heck!

It wasn't until we went to El Paso and visited his aunt Irma that I understood what he was talking about. I wasn't using nearly enough water when I cooked them and then later when I was working as a pastry chef in San Francisco, I watched my coworker shower her sofrito (caramelized onions, chiles, and garlic) with way more spice than I ever would have added. This aromatic broth the beans cook in is how they get all their flavor.

We typically make a big pot of beans and then eat them in different ways all week. The first night we ladle up bowls of the beans and broth and eat them as a soupy side dish. The next night we might use them to top our stuffed sweet potatoes (page 117) or fill our tacos. If there's any beans left by Saturday morning, we'll mash them up in oil to make refried beans for breakfast.

The instructions below work for dried pinto beans, Peruano beans, or black beans. You don't need to soak the beans for this recipe, but if you want to soak them overnight, it will cut the cook time down by 15 minutes.

❄ INSTRUCTIONS ❄

Place the black beans in a large bowl. Cover with water and swish the water around to rinse the beans. Pour them into a large colander and rinse once more, moving the beans around in the running water looking for pieces of dirt or small rocks.

Turn the Instant Pot to SAUTE on HI. Add the oil. Once the oil is hot, add the onion and sauté until just starting to become translucent. Add the garlic and serranos. Let them get a bit tender, then add the cumin, chile powder, coriander, and epazote. Sauté, stirring frequently, until the spices become toasted and fragrant. Add the tomatoes, beans, and water.

Continued >

Seal the Instant Pot. Select Pressure Cook HIGH (manual) for 30 minutes. It will take about 15 minutes for the machine to come up to pressure before the cooking cycle begins. When the 30 minutes of pressure cooking has finished, let the pressure release naturally for at least 20 minutes. Quick release the remaining pressure. Carefully open the lid.

Before adding any salt, check to see if the beans are tender. The beans should be easy to mash between your thumb and forefinger. If they are still hard, close the pot and cook them for 5 or 10 minutes. You'll need to let the pressure release naturally for at least 15 minutes before opening the pot once more, to prevent any liquid spurting out of the pressure cooker lid. Once they are cooked, stir in 1 tablespoon (15 g) of salt. Taste and add more, if needed. Enjoy the beans just like this as a soup or side.

Beans for Salad or Topping

To enjoy the beans in a salad or as a topping for the Loaded Sweet Potatoes (page 117) or to use in the Enchilada Casserole (page 111), remove with a slotted spoon leaving the broth behind and combine with other ingredients or use on their own. Save the bean broth and enjoy as a soup later.

Refried Beans

Set a strainer over a large heatproof bowl. Using kitchen mitts or towels, carefully remove the metal insert and drain the beans into the strainer, reserving the liquid. Rinse and dry the insert and return it to the pressure cooker. Set again to SAUTE on HI. Add 3 tablespoons (45 ml) of oil. Once the oil is hot, add the drained beans and 1 cup (235 ml) of the reserved bean broth. For chunky beans, mash with a potato masher until you reach the consistency you like. For smoother beans, use an immersion blender. Add as much liquid as necessary for smooth beans.

Turn the pressure cooker off and serve right away. Alternatively, turn to KEEP WARM, place the lid back on the pressure cooker, and keep warm for up to 1 hour.

INSTANT POT MOLE AMARILLO

INGREDIENTS

- ¼ cup (59 ml) avocado or sunflower oil
- ½ small white onion, chopped
- 3 cloves garlic, chopped
- 2 teaspoons (10 g) kosher salt, plus more to taste
- 2 medium guajillo chiles, stemmed, seeded, rinsed, and chopped
- 1 dried morita chile, stemmed, seeded, rinsed, and chopped
- 1 dried ancho chile, stemmed, seeded, rinsed, and chopped
- ½ cup (75 g) whole raw peanuts
- ¼ cup (35 g) raw pepitas
- 5 medium tomatillos, husks removed and rinsed
- 1½ cups (355 ml) water
- 1 large tomato, chopped
- 2 teaspoons (5 g) ground cumin
- ¼ teaspoon ground black pepper
- ¼ teaspoon ground allspice
- ¼ teaspoon ground cinnamon

SERVES 6 TO 8

The first thing you need to know about this mole amarillo, or yellow mole, is it is not yellow at all. So if you are looking down into your pot thinking you've done something wrong—you haven't. It *is* lighter in color than many other versions of mole, many of which contain hunks of bittersweet chocolate, blackened chiles, and charred vegetables.

This is a very pared down, simplified mole that can be made on any given weeknight. Granted, mole isn't a meal in and of itself, but it can be spooned over roasted vegetables, folded into warm tortillas (page 71), or ladled over a bowl of rice and beans for an impressive dinner in under thirty minutes. Use the sauce to make the enmoladas (page 71) or serve with Oven-Baked Garlic-Cilantro Rice (page 175) and Roasted Kabocha Squash (page 171).

❋ INSTRUCTIONS ❋

Turn the Instant Pot to SAUTE on HI. Add the oil and let it heat up for 1 to 2 minutes. Add the onion and garlic. Season with salt and cook, stirring occasionally, until it becomes translucent and soft.

Add the chiles, peanuts, and pepitas. Season again with salt and cook, stirring occasionally, until the chiles are toasted and are changing color, and the pepitas start to pop.

Add the remaining ingredients, including the 2 teaspoons (10 g) of salt. Seal the Instant Pot. Select Pressure Cook HIGH (manual) for 10 minutes. It will take about 15 minutes for the machine to come up to pressure before the cooking cycle begins. When the 10 minutes of pressure cooking has finished, quick release the pressure or let the pressure release naturally. Carefully open the lid.

Puree the ingredients until smooth with an immersion blender or transfer to a blender and blend until smooth. (Be careful blending hot liquids; see the note on page 103.) Taste and season with more salt as needed.

POWER-UP YOUR VEGGIES

●●●●●●●●●●●●●●●●●●●●●●●●●●●●●●●●●●●●●

Dried chiles are an excellent way to add flavor and a healthy kick to your diet. The capsaicin found in various levels in dried chiles gives them their fiery flavor and is also linked to heart health, a higher metabolism, and may even be an effective pain reliever. Cooking with dried chiles seems to cause some anxiety for some people, but they are painless friends. Simply remove the stem and tear open the chile to reveal its seeds. Remove all the seeds and rinse the chile under cold water to get rid of any dust or stray seeds. Then they are ready to use!

DRIED FAVA BEAN SOUP WITH MINT AND GUAJILLO CHILE-GARLIC OIL

INGREDIENTS

- 6 cloves garlic, thinly sliced
- 1 dried ancho chile, stemmed, seeded, rinsed, and thinly sliced
- 1¼ cups (295 ml) olive oil, divided
- ½ pound (225 g) dried fava beans
- 1 medium white onion, chopped
- 1 medium tomato, chopped
- ⅓ cup (6 g) chopped fresh cilantro (tender leaves and stems)
- 1 tablespoon (2 g) dried mint
- 2 bay leaves
- 5 cups (1.2 L) water
- 2 teaspoons (10 g) kosher salt, plus more to taste

SERVES 4 TO 6

One of the most delicious morsels I ate the last time my husband and I were in Mexico City was a torpedo-shaped blue corn masa cake stuffed with beans and cheese called a tlacoyo. Upon closer inspection, I was surprised to find the filling was fava beans and not a more widely used bean such as pinto or black beans.

Come to find out, fava beans, even though they are not native to Mexico, have a long history there and are enjoyed fresh and dried throughout the country. One of the most approachable and comforting ways is in a simple brothy soup drizzled with a not-at-all-spicy chile-garlic oil.

Puree the soup if you'd like, or leave it chunky—the choice is yours.

❋ INSTRUCTIONS ❋

Make the chile-garlic oil by combining the garlic, chile, and 1 cup (236 ml) of oil in a small saucepan. Bring to a boil over medium heat, then reduce the heat to low. Cook until the oil is infused with flavor, about 5 minutes. At first you'll only get the garlic smell, but then the chile will start coming through. Remove from the heat and let cool to room temperature.

Place the fava beans in a large bowl. Cover with water and swish the water around to rinse the beans. Pour into a large colander and rinse once more, moving the beans around in the running water looking for pieces of dirt or small rocks.

Turn the Instant Pot to SAUTE on HI. Add the remaining oil. Once the oil is hot, add the onion. Sauté for 6 to 8 minutes, until it

starts to caramelize and become golden brown. Add the fava beans, tomato, cilantro, mint, bay leaves, and water.

Seal the Instant Pot. Select Pressure Cook HIGH (manual) for 30 minutes. It will take about 15 minutes for the machine to come up to pressure before the cooking cycle begins. When the 30 minutes of pressure cooking has finished, let the pressure release naturally for at least 20 minutes. Quick release the remaining pressure. Carefully open the lid.

Remove the bay leaves, and add the salt. Puree with an immersion blender or transfer to a blender and puree until smooth. Be careful blending hot liquids (see the note on page 103). Season again with salt, if needed. Serve in bowls drizzled with the chile-garlic oil.

TECHNIQUE

•••••••••••••••••••••••••••••••••••

If you decide to puree this soup or any hot liquid in a blender, please be careful. Hot liquid plus blender on high equals a massive burning explosion. To do so safely, only fill the blender two-thirds of the way. Cover with the lid but remove the insert from the middle. Cover the lid with a couple paper towels folded several times and hold them over the lid with your hand the whole time. Start blending on low and increase the speed, until smooth.

POTATO SOUP WITH MELTY CHEESE AND TOASTED PEPITAS

INGREDIENTS

- 5 tablespoons (74 ml) olive oil, divided
- 1 medium white onion, diced
- 4 medium poblano peppers, stemmed, seeded, and diced
- 2 cloves garlic, chopped
- 2 teaspoons (10 g) kosher salt, plus more to taste
- A few pinches of freshly ground black pepper
- 5 large Yukon gold potatoes, peeled and diced (about 1½ pounds [680 g])
- 1 teaspoon dried Mexican oregano
- 6 cups (1.4 L) water
- ½ cup (70 g) raw pepitas
- 2 cups (226 g) shredded Oaxaca cheese
- 1 cup (100 g) sliced scallions

SERVES 4 TO 6

● ● ● ● ● ● ● ● ● ● ● ● ● ● ●

This potato soup defies all expectations. It is not a heavy chowder or overly cheesy. Your spoon will not stick up in your bowl. No, this potato soup has a gentle broth made from onion, garlic, waxy Yukon gold potatoes, and grassy poblano peppers. The richness only comes in the end when handfuls of milky Oaxaca cheese are added to each bowl. The hot, fragrant broth is ladled over the top and melts the cheese as it makes its way to the table, then scooped up with each nourishing spoonful.

Don't skip the toasted pepitas. Their crunch is a necessary contrast to an otherwise delicate soup.

❈ INSTRUCTIONS ❈

Turn the Instant Pot to SAUTE on HI. Add 4 tablespoons (59 ml) of the oil. Once the oil is hot, add the onion, poblanos, and garlic. Season with salt and black pepper. Sauté until the onions start to caramelize and become brown around the edges.

Add the potatoes, oregano, water, and 2 teaspoons (10 g) of the salt. Seal the Instant Pot. Select Pressure Cook HIGH (manual) for 10 minutes. It will take about 15 minutes for the machine to come up to pressure before the cooking cycle begins. When the 10 minutes of pressure cooking has finished, let the pressure release naturally for at least 10 minutes. Quick release the remaining pressure. Carefully open the lid.

Meanwhile, toast the pepitas by heating the remaining tablespoon (15 ml) of oil in a small frying pan over medium heat. Add the pepitas and toast, stirring frequently, until they turn golden brown and start to pop. Remove from the heat, sprinkle with salt, and set aside to cool.

Taste and season with more salt as needed. Divide the shredded cheese between the bowls, ladle the soup on top, then garnish with the toasted pepitas, scallions, and black pepper.

SMOKY TOMATO TORTILLA SOUP

INGREDIENTS

FOR THE SOUP

- 2 tablespoons (30 ml) olive oil
- 1 large white onion, chopped
- 3 cloves garlic, peeled and left whole
- 1 teaspoon kosher salt, plus more to taste
- 2 cans (15 ounces, or 425 g each) fire-roasted tomatoes
- 3 cups (705 ml) water
- 1 chipotle in adobo sauce
- 1 teaspoon dried Mexican oregano

FOR SERVING

- Tortilla strips (page 43) or store-bought tortilla chips
- 1 lime, cut into wedges
- 1 large, ripe avocado, peeled, pitted, and chopped

SERVES 4

This is the kind of low-maintenance dinner that can be made in minutes and everyone loves. No one, and I mean *no one*, turns down a bowl of tortilla soup.

The one thing an Instant Pot can't do is char things, so we'll need to sauté the onions and garlic in this recipe until they are as cooked as possible without the burn warning going off. This will get us as close to that irresistible smoky flavor you'd get from charring the vegetables over an open flame.

Fry up your own tortilla strips (page 43) or crumble store-bought tortilla chips on top.

❈ INSTRUCTIONS ❈

To make the soup: Turn the Instant Pot to SAUTE on HI. Add the oil and let it warm for 1 to 2 minutes. Add the onion and garlic. Season with salt and cook, stirring occasionally, until they are really dark, almost charred brown. Add the tomatoes, water, chipotle, oregano, and the teaspoon of measured salt.

Seal the Instant Pot. Select Pressure Cook HIGH (manual) for 10 minutes. It will take about 15 minutes for the machine to come up to pressure before the cooking cycle begins. When the 10 minutes of pressure cooking has finished, let the pressure release naturally for at least 10 minutes. Quick release the remaining pressure. Carefully open the lid

Puree with an immersion blender or transfer to a blender and puree until smooth. Be careful blending hot liquids (see the note on page 103). Taste and season with salt.

To serve: Ladle the soup into bowls and garnish with tortilla strips, a squeeze of lime, and hunks of avocado.

VEGAN RED POZOLE WITH MUSHROOMS

INGREDIENTS

FOR THE POZOLE

- 2 cans (24 ounces, or 680 g each) hominy
- 2 dried ancho chiles, stemmed, seeded, and rinsed
- 2 dried guajillo chiles, stemmed, seeded, and rinsed
- 1 medium white onion, chopped
- 3 cloves garlic, peeled and chopped
- 1 teaspoon ground cumin
- 2 whole cloves
- 1 tablespoon (15 g) kosher salt, plus more to taste
- ¼ cup (59 ml) olive oil, divided
- 2 pounds (907 g) cremini mushrooms, wiped clean, and sliced
- 6 cups (1.4 L) water

FOR SERVING

- ½ medium white onion, minced
- 2 tablespoons (6 g) dried Mexican oregano
- 2 limes, cut into wedges
- 5–6 thinly sliced radishes

SERVES 6 TO 8

Pozole is one of the most beloved and legendary dishes in Mexico. There are records of it as a celebratory meal dating as far back as the Aztecs. At its base is its namesake ingredient—pozole, which in Mexico is a specific type of field corn grown exclusively for this dish that is bigger and sweeter than the type grown for tortillas. Hominy is most widely used here in the United States, where our varieties of corn are severely limited in comparison.

Three types of pozole reflect the Mexican flag: red, white, and green. The white doesn't have an additional sauce added to it. The green is flavored with tomatillos, cilantro, and green chiles. The one we're making is a rich stew made with dried chiles.

The garnishes for pozole aren't optional; don't skip them and think it will be the same.

❀ INSTRUCTIONS ❀

To make the pozole: Drain the hominy and place it in a large bowl. Cover with water and let soak while you prepare the other ingredients. Cover the dried chiles with very hot water and let them soak until soft and pliable, about 10 to 15 minutes.

Remove the soaked chiles with tongs and save the soaking liquid. Add the chiles to a blender. Add the onion, garlic, cumin, cloves, salt, and ½ cup (120 ml) of the soaking liquid. Blend on high until smooth.

Turn the Instant Pot to SAUTE on HI. Add half the oil and let heat for 1 to 2 minutes. Add half the mushrooms, stir to coat in the oil, then let cook, undisturbed, until they are lightly golden brown on the bottom. Stir and let cook until beginning to soften. Remove to a plate, and repeat with the remaining oil and mushrooms.

Return all the mushrooms to the pot and add the blended chile mixture. Cook, stirring frequently, until the sauce has changed color to a dark red and is fragrant. Add the water and turn the Instant Pot off for a moment.

Continued >

TECHNIQUE

●●●●●●●●●●●●●●●●●●●●●●●●●●●●●●●●●●●●●●●

To get a nicely browned mushroom, you can't crowd the pan. Only put as many mushrooms as will fit in a single layer when sautéing them, otherwise they will just steam and become rubbery. Don't move them around too much either. Let them get a nice golden crust before giving the pot a stir. Never add salt to a sautéed mushroom until the very end. The salt causes them to release moisture and prevents them from browning.

Drain the hominy, give one last rinse, and add to the Instant Pot. Seal the Instant Pot. Select Pressure Cook HIGH (manual) for 10 minutes. It will take about 15 minutes for the machine to come up to pressure before the cooking cycle begins. When the 10 minutes of pressure cooking has finished, let the pressure release naturally for at least 10 minutes. Quick release the remaining pressure. Carefully open the lid. Taste and season with salt as needed.

To serve: Ladle into bowls and pass garnishes at the table for everyone to top their own bowls to their liking.

BLACK BEAN ENCHILADA CASSEROLE

INGREDIENTS

FOR THE ENCHILADA SAUCE

- 1 can (14 ounces, or 397 g) fire-roasted tomatoes
- 1 small white onion, chopped
- 2–3 chipotles in adobo sauce
- 2 cloves garlic, chopped
- 2 teaspoons (10 g) kosher salt
- 1 teaspoon dried Mexican oregano
- 1 teaspoon ground cumin

A version of this deeply satisfying cheesy casserole is the most-loved recipe on my blog. So, of course, I had to include it here! It took a few tries to adapt it for the Instant Pot. I swapped out the corn tortillas in the original recipe for crunchier tostadas that could stand up to the Instant Pot's steam. I also reduced the amount of some of the ingredients (a few attempts ended in very messy explosions) but the upside is this smart new recipe that takes half the time!

Have you ever made a casserole in an Instant Pot? You'll need a springform cake pan—make sure it's one that fits in your machine. As you layer all the ingredients it will seem like they will not fit, but just press down firmly as you go. The springform pan will be full, for sure, when you put it in the Instant Pot. Cover tightly with foil to prevent leaks and rest assured everything will cook down and reduce in size for a manageable, sliceable, and absolutely killer casserole.

Continued

INGREDIENTS

FOR THE ENCHILADAS

- 2 tablespoons (30 ml) olive oil
- 2 chayote squash, peeled, pitted, and chopped
- 2 small red bell peppers, cored, seeded, and chopped
- 1 red onion, half chopped, half thinly sliced
- 3 ounces (85 g) soft chèvre goat cheese, crumbled
- 10 ounces (280 g) grated manchego cheese (about 2½ cups grated)
- Kosher salt, to taste
- 8 (6-inch, or 15-cm) tostadas
- 2½ cups (440 g) Sofrito Black Beans (page 97) or 2 cans of black beans (15 ounces, or 425 g each), drained and rinsed
- ½ cup (8 g) chopped fresh cilantro (tender leaves and stems), plus more leaves for garnish
- 3 cloves garlic, minced

SERVES 8 TO 10

❉ INSTRUCTIONS ❉

To make the sauce: Combine all the ingredients in a blender, and blend until smooth. Taste and add another chipotle if you'd like it spicier. The sauce can be made up to 3 days in advance, covered and refrigerated until ready to use.

To make the enchiladas: Turn the Instant Pot to SAUTE on HI. Add the oil and let heat for 1 to 2 minutes. Add the chayote, bell peppers, and chopped onion. Season with salt and cook, stirring occasionally, until soft and translucent, about 10 minutes. Using kitchen mitts or towels, carefully remove the metal insert, scrape the vegetables onto a plate, and rinse and dry the insert.

Return the insert to the Instant Pot, pour in 2 cups (475 ml) of cold water, and place the metal trivet in the bottom of the pot.

Mix the goat cheese and manchego cheese in a medium bowl.

Grease a 6- or 7-inch (15- or 18-cm) springform cake pan (check to make sure it will fit in your Instant Pot). Cover the bottom with ½ cup (120 ml) sauce, then place 2 tostadas on top, breaking into large pieces so they cover as much of the pan as possible

Top with a quarter of the sautéed vegetables, a quarter of the black beans, a quarter of the cheese mixture, a quarter of the cilantro, and a quarter of the garlic. Sprinkle with salt. When layering, spread the ingredients so they cover as much of the dish as possible.

Keep layering, starting with ½ cup (120 ml) of sauce and continuing with the ingredients in the order listed until all the ingredients are used, and press down on the layers as you build so they will fit in the dish. Cover tightly with foil.

Place the pan on top of the trivet in the Instant Pot, cover with the lid, and seal. Select Pressure Cook HIGH (manual) for 10 minutes. It will take about 15 minutes for the machine to come up to pressure before the cooking cycle begins. When the 10 minutes of pressure cooking has finished, let the pressure release naturally for at least 10 minutes. Quick release the remaining pressure. Carefully open the lid.

Using oven mitts or kitchen towels, remove the springform pan from the Instant Pot. Let sit 10 minutes before cutting. Remove the foil, run a knife around the edge of the pan, then remove the side. Top with red onion slices and cilantro. Slice and serve.

POWER-UP YOUR VEGGIES

Chayote is a pear-shaped squash with the texture somewhere between jicama and zucchini. It is low in calories and packed with nutrients and tons of fiber. It can be eaten raw or cooked and is easy to work with (as long as you buy them without the pokey spines). Simply cut in half and chop. The peel can be eaten but sometimes is tough, so I like to peel them first. There is a soft, little seed in the middle that is so tender it's inconsequential, but scoop it out with a spoon if you want.

MEXICAN RICE BOWLS WITH BOILED EGGS AND AVOCADO PICO DE GALLO

INGREDIENTS

- 6 large eggs
- 1½ cups (278 g) white jasmine rice
- 1 can (15 ounces, or 425 g) fire-roasted tomatoes
- ½ small white onion, chopped
- 1 medium jalapeño, stemmed, seeds removed if you'd like it less spicy
- 2 cloves garlic, chopped
- 2 teaspoons kosher salt, divided, plus more to taste
- ¼ cup (59 ml) avocado or sunflower oil
- 2 large, ripe avocados, peeled, pitted, and diced
- ¼ medium red onion, minced
- 1 serrano chile, stemmed, seeded (if you'd like it less spicy), and minced
- ½ cup (8 g) chopped fresh cilantro (tender leaves and stems)
- ¼ cup (60 ml) fresh lime juice (from 2 limes)

SERVES 4 TO 6

Red rice, Spanish rice, Mexican rice, no matter what you call it, it all equals the same thing: love. Along with my mother-in-law's picadillo, her rice is what all the grandkids crave. "Nana's rice." They say those two words with such passion you'd think they were taking some sort of holy vow.

It's with this spirit of cozy, comforting love I give you this Mexican rice bowl. It's like a big edible hug with rosy red rice, hard-cooked eggs (as jammy as you'd like them), and a big dollop of creamy avocado (with fresh, crunchy onions and jalapeños for texture). Best part? All cooked in mere minutes in the Instant Pot! Serve with Sofrito Black Beans (page 97) for a more substantial meal.

❄ INSTRUCTIONS ❄

Add 1 cup (235 ml) of water to the Instant Pot. Place the metal trivet into the pot and the eggs on top of the trivet. Cover with the lid and seal. Select Pressure Cook HIGH (manual) for 2 to 6 minutes depending on how cooked you like your eggs. It will take about 15 minutes for the machine to come up to pressure before the cooking cycle begins. When the desired time of pressure cooking has finished, quick release the pressure. Carefully open the lid, remove the eggs, and set aside while you cook the rice.

Rinse out the Instant Pot insert and dry well. Return it to the Instant Pot. Combine the tomatoes, onion, jalapeño, garlic, and salt in a blender. Blend on high until smooth.

Turn the Instant Pot to SAUTE on HI. Add the oil and let heat for 1 to 2 minutes. Add the rice and fry in the oil, stirring frequently, until

golden brown and toasted. Add the blended tomato sauce, and stir to combine.

Seal the Instant Pot. Select Pressure Cook HIGH (manual) for 4 minutes. It will take about 15 minutes for the machine to come up to pressure before the cooking cycle begins. When the 4 minutes of pressure cooking has finished, let the pressure release naturally for at least 5 minutes. Quick release the remaining pressure. Carefully open the lid.

Meanwhile, stir together the avocado pico de gallo by combining the avocados, onion, serrano, lime juice, and salt in a medium bowl. Gently stir to combine. Taste and add more salt, if needed.

Scoop the rice into bowls. Peel 1 to 2 eggs, cut in half, and set them on top of the rice along with a spoonful of avocado pico de gallo.

LOADED SWEET POTATOES WITH LIME CREMA, SOFRITO BEANS, ROASTED KALE, AND CHIVES

INGREDIENTS

- 1 cup (235 ml) water
- 4–8 sweet potatoes (depending on the size), scrubbed well and pierced with a fork several times all over
- 1 cup (230 g) crema agria (page 23) or sour cream
- 1 teaspoon lime zest
- 2 tablespoons (28 ml) lime juice (from 1 lime)
- ½ teaspoon kosher salt
- 1 cup (150 g) crumbled goat cheese
- 2½ cups (xx g) Sofrito Black Beans (page 97) or 1 recipe canned black beans (page 182)
- ½ cup (24 g) chopped chives
- 1 recipe Chipotle-Garlic Roasted Kale (page 175)
- 1 lime, cut into wedges

SERVES 4 TO 8

This is a super fun dinner that will get your kids to eat a surprising amount of vegetables: a sweet potato bar! I find when I lay out all the toppings—crispy-edged roasted kale, creamy black beans, fresh chives, basically anything else you want to add—and let my kids top their own potato, they eat way more of it than if I had decorated it myself. It is an unsuspecting way to shove as many nutrients as possible into your child, but you didn't hear it from me.

A note about cooking sweet potatoes in an Instant Pot: Most important, use the same-sized potatoes. There's a shorter cooking time for small potatoes and a longer cooking time for larger potatoes: For a small (6–8 ounces, or 168–225 g) sweet potato, set the time for 10 minutes. For a medium (8–12 ounces, or 225–340 g) sweet potato, 16 minutes. For a large (12–16 ounces, or 340–455 g) sweet potato, 22 minutes.

❈ INSTRUCTIONS ❈

Add 1 cup (235 ml) of water to the Instant Pot. Place the metal trivet into the pot and the sweet potatoes on top of the trivet. Cover with the lid and seal. Select Pressure Cook HIGH (manual) for 12 to 25 minutes depending on the size of your sweet potatoes (see headnote). It will take about 15 minutes for the machine to come up to pressure before the cooking cycle begins. When the desired time of pressure cooking has finished, let the pressure release naturally for at least 10 minutes. Quick release the remaining pressure. Carefully open the lid.

Meanwhile, combine the crema, lime zest, lime juice, and salt. Whisk until smooth.

Halve each potato, and place in a serving dish. Use a fork to gently mash. Set out a make-your-own sweet potato bar with goat cheese, black beans, lime crema, chives, and kale. Let everyone top their own potato. Squeeze with lime wedges and eat!

5
FROM THE GRILL

BEING BLESSED TO LIVE IN SOUTHERN CALIFORNIA MEANS WE GRILL ALL YEAR LONG, WHICH IS WONDERFUL BECAUSE COOKING THIS WAY (IDEALLY OVER MESQUITE CHARCOAL) IS THE ESSENCE OF MANY MEXICAN DISHES.

Without cooking over an open fire it's difficult to re-create authentic recipes with a signature smoky flavor at home. So, fire up your grill (or grill pan for you city dwellers or those living with bad weather)!

Vegetables love the grill and this section will hopefully convince you that you can and should grill any vegetable (or fruit). There are a few things to remember when grilling vegetables for the best results. First, slice the vegetables into the same thickness so they cook at the same rate. Next, make sure your grill is hot (350° to 450°F [175° to 230°C]) and your grill grates are clean and oiled before you add your veggies. Last, the easiest way to control the fire and flare-ups is to grill with the lid closed.

AL PASTOR WINTER SQUASH WITH CHARRED POBLANO CASHEW CREAM

INGREDIENTS

FOR THE CASHEW CREAM

- 1 cup (137 g) raw, unsalted cashews
- 2¾ cups (645 ml) water, divided
- 2 large poblano peppers
- ½ teaspoon kosher salt

FOR THE SQUASH

- 1 large butternut squash
- 2 dried guajillo chiles, stemmed, seeded, and rinsed
- 1¾ ounces (50 g) achiote paste
- ½ cup (80 g) chopped white onion
- 8 cloves garlic, chopped
- 3 tablespoons (45 ml) apple cider vinegar
- 1 teaspoon ground black pepper
- 1 teaspoon dried Mexican oregano
- 1 teaspoon kosher salt
- ½ teaspoon ground allspice
- ½ teaspoon ground cumin
- ½ teaspoon ground cinnamon
- 8–10 (6-inch, or 15-cm) warm corn tortillas

SERVES 4

If you've ever seen the tall cylindrical rotisseries of meat (typically pork) ubiquitous at taco trucks and thought of shawarma, you were spot-on. Mexican cooks quickly adapted this way of cooking from Lebanese immigrants who moved to the country in the beginning of the twentieth century and Al Pastor was born!

This version takes that delicious Al Pastor marinade of achiote, dried chiles, and garlic, and uses it to flavor meaty hunks of winter squash that get slowly charred on the grill. The best way to enjoy it is sandwiched in a warm tortilla, topped with cooling (and vegan) poblano cashew cream.

There aren't very many plan-ahead recipes in this book, but this is one of them. The cashew cream and squash are best if they're started a day before you'd like to eat them.

❊ INSTRUCTIONS ❊

To make the cashew cream: Place the cashews in a medium bowl and cover with 2 cups (475 ml) of water. Soak at room temperature for 10 to 12 hours, or until they break apart when pressed between your finger and thumb.

The next day, place the poblano peppers directly over a gas flame (if you have a gas stove) or under the broiler set to high. Char the peppers until the skin is blackened all over. Remove to a heatproof bowl and cover with plastic wrap. Let sit until cool enough to handle.

Peel the blackened skin off by rubbing it with your fingers, then remove the stem and seeds. Rinse under cold water to get any last bits of skin and seeds off. Give the peppers a quick chop.

Drain the cashews and add them to a blender with the remaining ¾ cup (175 ml) of water, the poblanos, and salt. Blend on high until very smooth.

To make the squash: With a sharp chef's knife, cut the long end from the bulb end of the butternut squash. Remove the stem ends, then peel off the tough skin with a vegetable peeler. Cut the bulb section in half vertically, scoop out the seeds and strings with a large spoon, then cut into ½-inch (1-cm)-thick slices. Cut the long end in half vertically and slice into ½-inch (1-cm)-thick half-moon slices.

Continued >

Bring a large pot of salted water to a boil. Add the squash pieces and cook for 8 to 10 minutes, or until barely tender when poked with a sharp paring knife. They should still be a bit crunchy in the middle. Drain, rinse with cold water to stop the cooking, and drain again. Place in a large baking dish or other container big enough to hold all the squash at once.

Heat a comal or cast-iron skillet over medium heat for at least 3 minutes, or until hot but not smoking. Toast the guajillo chiles, rotating frequently with tongs for 2 to 3 minutes. Remove them from the heat as soon as they start to smell nutty, but before they burn or blister.

Meanwhile, bring a small saucepan full of water to a boil over high heat. Place the toasted chiles in the boiling water, pushing down to submerge. Remove from the heat and let soak until very tender, about 15 to 20 minutes.

Remove the soaked chiles with tongs and save the soaking liquid. Add the chiles to a blender. Add the achiote paste, onion, garlic, vinegar, black pepper, oregano, salt, allspice, cumin, cinnamon, and ½ cup (120 ml) of the soaking liquid. Blend on high until very smooth. The marinade should be a pourable consistency but thick enough to coat the squash. If it is too thick, add ¼ cup (60 ml) more soaking liquid and blend again.

Pour over the squash, tossing to coat well. Cover, refrigerate, and marinate for at least 2 hours or up to 12.

When ready to grill, heat a grill to medium heat (350° to 450°F [175° to 230°C]). Clean the grates and brush with oil. Grill the marinated squash, flipping when grill marks appear and the squash has softened slightly, 7 to 8 minutes per side. Remove from the heat and arrange in a shallow serving dish. Cover tightly with aluminum foil to keep warm and let steam, covered, for 10 minutes. Serve with warm tortillas and the poblano cashew cream.

SANGRIA-MARINATED VEGGIE SKEWERS

Why drink your sangria when you can eat it? Just kidding—obviously drinking sangria is preferred, but the ingredients that make a delicious sangria double as a pretty exquisite marinade. The veggies listed below scream summer, but cold-weather alternatives such as Brussels sprouts, cauliflower, and broccoli work too. Whatever you do, don't skip the grilled lemons; they add that special finishing touch.

Continued >

INGREDIENTS

- 1 cup (235 ml) white wine
- 2 tablespoons (28 ml) fresh orange juice (from 1 orange)
- 2 tablespoons (30 ml) olive oil
- 1 tablespoon (15 ml) orange liqueur, such as Cointreau
- 1 teaspoon kosher salt
- ½ teaspoon ground black pepper
- 2 lemons
- 1 large ear corn, husks removed
- 1 medium zucchini
- 1 medium yellow summer squash
- ½ medium red bell pepper, seeded and cored
- ½ large red onion
- 8 button mushrooms, wiped clean
- 1 recipe Oven-Baked Garlic-Cilantro Rice (page 175)
- 1 recipe Ancho Chile Crema (page 77)
- 8–10 (6-inch, or 15-cm) warm flour tortillas

SERVES 4

❀ INSTRUCTIONS ❀

If using wooden skewers, prepare them by soaking in water for 30 minutes while you prepare the vegetables. If using metal skewers, no prep is necessary.

Whisk together the wine, orange juice, oil, orange liqueur, salt, and black pepper in a large bowl. Cut the lemons and the vegetables into 1-inch (2.5-cm) slices or chunks. Toss to coat in the marinade, and let marinate for at least 15 minutes or up to 1 hour.

Thread the lemon slices and the vegetables on the skewers, alternating the veggies, until you've reached the end of the skewer.

Heat a grill to medium heat (350° to 450°F [175° to 230°C]). Clean the grates and brush with oil. Grill the vegetables with the lid closed until tender and lightly charred, turning and brushing with leftover marinade every 3 to 5 minutes. Serve warm or at room temperature, squeezing the grilled lemon slices over the veggies.

Serve with Oven-Baked Garlic-Cilantro Rice (page 175), Ancho Chile Crema (page 77), and warm tortillas.

CHIPOTLE-SPICED GRILLED CAULIFLOWER TACOS WITH PICKLED RED ONIONS

INGREDIENTS

FOR THE PICKLED RED ONIONS

- 1 medium red onion, thinly sliced
- ½ cup (120 ml) distilled white vinegar
- ½ cup (120 ml) water
- ¼ cup (50 g) granulated sugar
- ½ teaspoon kosher salt

FOR THE TACOS

- 1 large head cauliflower, leaves removed and sliced into 1-inch (2.5-cm)-thick slices
- ¼ cup (59 ml) olive oil
- 2 teaspoons (5 g) smoked paprika
- 1 teaspoon ground cumin
- ½–1 teaspoon chipotle powder (depending on how spicy you like things)
- ½ teaspoon kosher salt
- ½ teaspoon garlic powder

FOR SERVING

- 8–10 (6-inch, or 15-cm) warm corn tortillas
- ½ cup (8 g) chopped fresh cilantro (tender leaves and stems)
- 1 large, ripe avocado, peeled, pitted, and sliced
- 1 lime, sliced into wedges

SERVES 4

This might be a bold statement, but I think a perfectly charred cauliflower taco might be the most delicious taco you can eat. The rubble-edge of a head of cauliflower (especially one doused in chipotle spice) gets shatteringly crisp on the grill while the inside stays tender. Once you chop it into bite-sized pieces you get both parts in the same tremendously satisfying bite.

Along with a heap of warm tortillas and the pickled red onions you can add as many other toppings as you like. I suggest ripe avocado wedges (for creamy contrast), but a soothing salsita is never a bad idea. Try tomatillo-avocado salsa (page 73) or even a drizzle of Mexican crema.

❋ INSTRUCTIONS ❋

To make the pickled red onions: Place the onions in a medium heatproof bowl. Combine the vinegar, water, sugar, and salt in a small saucepan. Bring to a boil over medium heat, stirring until the sugar is dissolved. Remove from the heat, and pour over the red onions. Let cool to room temperature. Transfer to a mason jar or other container, seal, and refrigerate for up to 2 weeks.

To make the tacos: Heat a grill to medium heat (350° to 450°F [175° to 230°C]). Clean the grates and brush with oil. Arrange the cauliflower slices in a single layer on a baking sheet. Combine the oil, smoked paprika, cumin, chipotle powder, salt, and garlic powder in a small bowl. Drizzle over the cauliflower and rub it in so it gets in all the nooks and crannies.

Place the cauliflower on the grill and brush with any remaining marinade from the pan as it cooks. Grill for 3 to 5 minutes per side, or until grill marks form and it is tender when you pierce it with a fork.

To serve: Cut the grilled cauliflower into small bite-sized pieces. Serve with the pickled red onions, warm tortillas, lime wedges, cilantro, and avocado for topping.

TECHNIQUE

The easiest way to grill cauliflower is by cutting it into "steaks" or large, thick slices cut through the entire head of cauliflower. Remove the outer leaves and trim the stem end so it lies flat on your cutting board. Cut the cauliflower head in half, right through the middle. Then cut each half into two or three 1-inch (2.5-cm)-thick slices, depending on the size of your head of cauliflower. The small edges are a chef snack for you!

MEZCAL-MARINATED MUSHROOM AND EGGPLANT FAJITAS

INGREDIENTS

FOR THE ARBOL CHILE SALSA

- 2 tablespoons (30 ml) avocado or sunflower oil
- ½ medium white onion, sliced
- 5 cloves garlic, peeled
- 2 medium tomatoes, cored and quartered
- 3 dried arbol chiles, stemmed, and rinsed
- ⅓ cup (80 ml) water
- ½ teaspoon salt, plus more to taste

FOR THE FAJITAS

- ¼ cup (60 ml) mezcal
- ¼ cup (59 ml) olive oil
- 2 cloves garlic, minced
- 2 tablespoons (28 ml) fresh lime juice (from 1 lime)
- 1 tablespoon (5 g) Magic Spice Mix! (page 19)
- 1 teaspoon kosher salt
- 12 ounces (340 g) portobello mushrooms, stems removed and rubbed clean with a damp paper towel
- 1 pound (455 g) Japanese eggplant, trimmed and sliced vertically into ½-inch (1-cm)-thick strips (about 4 small)

FOR SERVING

- 8–10 (8-inch, or 20-cm) warm flour tortillas
- Lime Crema (page 85) or Mexican crema (page 23) (optional)
- 1 lime, cut into wedges

SERVES 4

● ● ● ● ● ● ● ● ● ● ● ● ● ● ●

Fajitas are more Texan than Mexican, but the allure of mezcal-marinated, grilled vegetables tucked inside a warm tortilla is universal. Shy away from using large globe eggplant if possible. Japanese, Chinese, or heirloom Italian varieties are much more flavorful and have much better texture for grilling. Summertime farmers' markets have the best selection of eggplant, so look there for some interesting options.

Don't let the mushrooms and eggplant sit in the marinade for too long or they will fall apart when you try to grill them. Marinating for 30 minutes to an hour is plenty of time. The fiery arbol chile salsa makes these fajitas complete. You can make it up to 3 days in advance and keep covered in the refrigerator.

❉ INSTRUCTIONS ❉

To make the salsa: Heat the oil in a medium frying pan over medium-high heat. Add the onions and garlic, and season with salt. Cook, stirring occasionally, until the onions and garlic are deeply caramelized and golden brown. Add the tomatoes and chiles, and season again with salt. Cook until the tomatoes are soft and caramelized in spots. Transfer everything to the blender. Add the water and salt. Blend on high until very smooth. Taste and add more salt, if needed.

To make the fajitas: Combine the mezcal, olive oil, garlic, lime juice, Magic Spice Mix!, and salt in a small bowl. Layer the mushrooms and eggplant in a shallow dish. Pour the marinade over the top and toss to coat thoroughly. Let the mixture marinate for 30 minutes. Once the mushrooms and eggplant are ready, heat a grill to medium heat (350° to 450°F [175° to 230°C]). Clean the grates and brush with oil.

When the grill is hot, add the mushrooms and eggplant (save the dish with the marinade in it). Grill until nicely charred on both sides. The eggplant takes 5 minutes, the mushrooms more like 10. Watch closely and flip once or twice to prevent them from getting burnt and brush the mushrooms and eggplant with the leftover marinade every time you turn them. You want to see grill marks, but they shouldn't be blackened. Move the eggplant to the side to keep warm while the mushrooms finish cooking.

To serve: Cut the mushrooms and eggplant into bite-sized strips, then return to the dish and toss in any leftover marinade. Tuck the grilled veggies into warm tortillas. Serve with the arbol chile salsa, crema (if using), and lime wedges for squeezing over your tacos.

POWER-UP YOUR VEGGIES

Did you know that there's more potassium in a portobello mushroom than a banana? It's true! These nutrient-rich foods are a great meat alternative because of their texture and earthy flavor. To clean them, rub the outside with a damp paper towel. Never clean them under running water, which will make them soggy and rubbery.

GRILLED VEGETABLE SALAD WITH HERBED REQUESÓN AND CITRUS VINAIGRETTE

INGREDIENTS

- 2 medium sweet potatoes, peeled and cut into ½-inch (1-cm)-thick wedges
- 2 hearts of romaine, cut in half
- 1 pound (455 g) asparagus, trimmed
- 1 medium zucchini, trimmed and cut vertically into ½-inch (1-cm)-thick slices
- 1 medium summer squash, trimmed and cut vertically into ½-inch (1-cm)-thick slices
- 1 small red onion, trimmed and cut into ½-inch (1-cm)-thick rings
- ¼ cup (59 ml) extra-virgin olive oil, divided
- 4 ounces (115 g) requesón
- 1 teaspoon minced Mexican tarragon or French tarragon
- 1 teaspoon minced fresh dill
- 1 teaspoon kosher salt, divided, plus more to taste
- ½ teaspoon ground black pepper, divided, plus more to taste
- 2 tablespoons (28 ml) fresh lime juice (from 1 lime)
- 2 tablespoons (28 ml) fresh tangerine juice (from 1 tangerine)
- 1 teaspoon lime zest
- 1 teaspoon tangerine zest
- ½ teaspoon ground coriander
- 4 large radishes, thinly sliced
- ½ cup (8 g) fresh cilantro (tender leaves and stems)

SERVES 4

This is a very fork-and-knife type of salad meant to impress a meat-eating guest (or partner) who may be misguided into thinking eating a plant-based meal leaves you unsatisfied. The key is cutting the vegetables into fat, steak fry–like wedges. These thicker pieces mean you can leave them on the grill a bit longer to get some real char without them disintegrating into mush.

Creamy requesón is the perfect partner to these deeply golden grilled veggies. It is a soft Mexican fresh cheese, similar to ricotta. You're not likely to find requesón at your local grocery store, unless your local grocery store specializes in Latin ingredients. You'll have to make a special trip to the Latin market—but while you're there, pick up that bunch of Mexican tarragon, cilantro, and the crunchiest radishes in town!

❀ INSTRUCTIONS ❀

Heat a grill to medium heat (350° to 450°F [175° to 230°C]). Clean the grates and brush with oil. Arrange the sweet potatoes, romaine, asparagus, zucchini, summer squash, and onions in a single layer on a baking sheet. Drizzle the vegetables with 2 tablespoons (30 ml) of the oil, and sprinkle evenly with salt and pepper.

Combine the requesón, tarragon, dill, ¼ teaspoon salt, and a pinch of black pepper in a small bowl. Mash with a fork to mix well.

Whisk together the lime and tangerine zest and juice, coriander, remaining salt, and remaining black pepper in a small bowl. Slowly drizzle in the remaining oil while whisking constantly until fully incorporated.

Grill the vegetables with the lid closed until tender and lightly charred all over, about 15 minutes for the sweet potatoes; 12 minutes for the onions; 5 to 7 minutes for the summer squash, zucchini, romaine, and asparagus.

Arrange the grilled vegetables on a large platter. Drop spoonfuls of the requesón here and there, sprinkle with the radishes and cilantro leaves. Drizzle with the dressing and serve.

STUFFED POBLANOS WITH CINNAMON-SCENTED STICKY RICE, GOAT CHEESE, AND MINT

Chiles rellenos are one of the most beloved Mexican dishes around. If you're looking for a more traditional version (in flavor, not preparation), check out the One-Pan Cheesy Rice Chile Relleno Casserole on page 154.

These grilled stuffed peppers are made with Mexican ingredients (poblano peppers, Cotija cheese, sweet corn), but take on a decidedly California tone. In fact, these peppers are a version of ones I learned to make when I was the sous chef at Mustards Grill in Napa Valley.

I love these peppers so much I make them as often as my family will let me. The grassy poblanos, chewy and fragrant cinnamon rice, a bit of sweetness from pops of corn, and lots of herbs and cheese: they are a meal all by themselves.

It may seem nuts to grill stuffed peppers by laying them on their sides, but trust me, I've made them a million times. The stuffing is so sticky, nothing is coming out.

Continued

INGREDIENTS

- ½ cup (100 g) uncooked white short-grain rice (like arborio or sushi rice)
- 1 cup (235 ml) water
- ¼ stick Ceylon cinnamon
- 1 teaspoon kosher salt, plus more to taste
- 4 medium poblano peppers
- 1 ear sweet corn, kernels removed, or 1 cup (164 g) frozen corn kernels (you need not thaw first)
- ½ cup (50 g) grated Cotija cheese
- ¼ cup (7.5 g) chopped fresh mint
- 1 tablespoon (4 g) chopped fresh dill
- 1 tablespoon (4 g) chopped fresh Italian parsley
- 1½ tablespoons (25 ml) fresh lemon juice (from 1 lemon)
- ¼ teaspoon ground black pepper
- 3 ounces (85 g) crumbled goat cheese
- Chipotle-Piloncillo Salsa (page 69)

SERVES 4

❀ INSTRUCTIONS ❀

Rinse the rice in a colander until the water runs clear. Combine the rice, water, cinnamon stick, and salt in a medium saucepan. Bring to a boil over high heat. Cover the pan and reduce the heat to low; cook until the water has been completely absorbed, about 15 to 20 minutes. Remove the lid from the pan, discard the cinnamon stick, and set the pan aside to let the rice cool. Meanwhile, prepare the peppers.

Use a paring knife to cut a wide circle around each stem (like when carving a jack-o'-lantern), so you end up with a cap that can be replaced once you've stuffed the peppers; be careful not to puncture or rip the peppers. Remove and discard any seeds and membranes from the cap and from the interior; set the peppers aside.

Once the rice is cool enough to handle, scrape it into a large bowl and add the corn kernels, Cotija, mint, dill, parsley, lemon juice, and pepper. Add in the crumbled goat cheese and gently fold in, trying not to break the cheese up too much. Taste and, if necessary, add more salt and black pepper.

Divide the rice mixture into 4 equal portions. Stuff each pepper with the filling, replace the caps, and press each cap into the filling. Pierce 2 toothpicks through each cap and out the sides of the pepper to secure the caps while on the grill; set aside until ready to cook. If you're stuffing the peppers more than 30 minutes before grilling, cover and refrigerate them for up to 4 hours. Let the peppers sit at room temperature at least 30 minutes before grilling so they cook faster and more evenly.

Heat the grill to medium-low heat (300° to 350°F [150° to 175°C]). Place the stuffed peppers on their sides and close the lid. Roll each pepper a quarter turn every few minutes to cook all sides. The peppers are finished once the filling is hot, the skins are well-charred, and the flesh is soft to the touch, about 15 minutes. Remove the toothpicks.

Pass Chipotle-Piloncillo Salsa at the table.

GRILLED AVOCADOS AND CHEESY GREEN CHILE GRITS WITH PICO DE GALLO

INGREDIENTS

FOR THE PICO DE GALLO

- 2 large, ripe tomatoes, cored and chopped
- ¼ medium red onion, minced
- 2 medium jalapeños, stemmed and minced (remove seeds if you'd like it less spicy)
- ¼ cup (4 g) chopped fresh cilantro (tender leaves and stems)
- ¼ cup (60 ml) plus 1 tablespoon (15 ml) fresh lime juice (from 3 limes), divided

FOR THE GRITS AND AVOCADOS

- 2 cups (475 ml) whole milk
- 2 cups (475 ml) water
- 1 teaspoon kosher salt, plus more to taste
- 1 cup (148 g) quick grits
- ¼ cup (55 g) unsalted butter
- 1 can (4 ounces, or 115 g) diced green chiles, drained
- 1½ cups (5 ounces, or 180 g) shredded aged white Cheddar cheese
- ½ teaspoon ground black pepper
- 2 large, ripe avocados, pitted
- 1 tablespoon (15 ml) olive oil

SERVES 4

To be sure, grits are not Mexican, but there is something deeply comforting and familiar to a bowl of creamy stone-ground field corn. And if you've never grilled an avocado before, you might be more tempted to do so if it will be served on top of a cheesy bowl of grits. Grilling an avocado may seem fussy and unnecessary and I hear you, but one bite of a fire-kissed avocado and you'll be convinced that every avocado from this point forward must be grilled.

The pico de gallo recipe is my go-to. Make it when tomatoes are at their peak, and if they're not, it's nothing a little extra lime juice, salt, and (gasp!) a pinch of sugar can't handle.

❋ INSTRUCTIONS ❋

To make the pico de gallo: Stir together the tomatoes, onion, jalapeños, cilantro, and ¼ cup (60 ml) of lime juice in a medium bowl. Season with salt and stir.

To make the grits and avocados: In a large saucepan, bring the milk, water, and 1 teaspoon of salt to a boil over medium-high heat. Once the milk mixture comes to a boil, slowly pour in the grits while continually whisking. Once all of the grits have been incorporated, decrease the heat to low and cover. Remove the lid and whisk frequently, every 1 to 2 minutes with a wire whisk, to prevent the grits from sticking or forming lumps; make sure to get into the corners of the saucepan when stirring. Cook for 5 minutes, or until the mixture is creamy.

Add the butter and green chiles. Stir until the butter is completely melted and incorporated, then stir in the cheese and black pepper. Taste and add more salt, if needed. Cover and remove from the heat.

Heat a grill to medium heat (350° to 450°F [175° to 230°C]). Clean the grates and brush with oil. Brush the avocado halves with oil and grill, cut-side down, until grill marks form and the avocado is warmed through, about 5 minutes. Remove from the grill, scoop the avocado halves out of their skin and cut each piece in half. Drizzle with the remaining lime juice and season with salt.

Spoon the warm grits into each bowl, arrange avocado pieces on top, and serve with pico de gallo.

QUESO ASADO WITH GRILLED CALABACITAS AND SALSA VERDE

INGREDIENTS

FOR THE QUESO AND CALABACITAS

- 1 package (10 ounces, or 280 g) panela cheese
- 2 medium calabacitas, or Mexican gray squash, ends trimmed and cut vertically into ½-inch (1-cm)-thick slices
- 2 bunches cherry tomatoes on the vine (about 8 ounces [225 g])
- 1 medium red onion, cut into ½-inch (1-cm)-thick rings
- 1 medium poblano pepper, stemmed, cut in half vertically and seeded
- ¼ cup (59 ml) olive oil
- 3 cloves garlic, minced
- 2 teaspoons (10 g) kosher salt
- 1 teaspoon minced fresh Mexican oregano or ½ teaspoon dried Mexican oregano
- ¼ teaspoon ground black pepper
- ¼ teaspoon ground cumin

FOR SERVING

- Salsa Verde (page 82)
- 8–10 (6-inch, or 15-cm) warm corn tortillas

SERVES 4

Calabacitas refers to a type of summer squash as well as a cherished Mexican side dish. Whenever we see the bins of sage green striped squash at our local Latin market, my husband always comments that his family ate them practically every single night when he was growing up.

Calabacitas (the side dish) is a combination of calabacitas (the squash), tomatoes, onion, and peppers sautéed until tender and then folded with cheese. This recipe takes all these elements to the grill for a showstopper of a protein-packed, plant-powered dinner.

❀ INSTRUCTIONS ❀

To make the queso and calabacitas: Heat a grill to medium heat (350° to 450°F [175° to 230°C]). Clean the grates and brush with oil. Arrange the cheese, squash, cherry tomatoes, onion, and pepper slices in a single layer on a baking sheet.

Combine the oil, garlic, salt, oregano, black pepper, and cumin in a small bowl. Pour over the cheese and vegetables, and rub the marinade in with your hands to cover all the surfaces.

Grill the vegetables with the lid on for 8 to 10 minutes, turning occasionally once grill marks form on one side. The tomatoes will take a bit less time, more like 5 to 6 minutes. Arrange on a platter.

Grill the panela cheese until nicely charred on one side, about 2 to 3 minutes. Flip with a metal spatula and grill until charred on the other side. It should be soft when you press on it but not runny. Place on the platter with the vegetables.

To serve: Cut the calabacitas, red onion, and poblano pepper into bite-sized pieces and the cheese in slices. Serve with the Salsa Verde and warm tortillas.

POWER-UP YOUR VEGGIES

Calabacitas, or Mexican gray squash, are a stocky summer squash with striped sage green skin and solid, crisp flesh. It has a plethora of vitamins, important for heart health, including vitamins A, C, and K as well as folate, manganese, and potassium. I love cooking with this particular variety of summer squash because the seeds are small, and the flesh is compact. Try it raw, sliced very thinly with a drizzle of good olive oil, a sprinkle of salt, and the zest and juice of a lime.

GRILLED ASPARAGUS AND BROCCOLINI WITH PEPITA PESTO AND RUNNY EGGS

INGREDIENTS

- ¾ cup (25 g) packed fresh mint, plus more for garnish
- ½ cup (10 g) packed fresh cilantro (tender leaves and stems)
- ¼ cup (18 g) raw pepitas
- 1 clove garlic
- ½ teaspoon kosher salt, plus more to taste
- ½ cup (118 ml) olive oil, divided
- 2 tablespoons (28 ml) fresh lemon juice (from 1 lemon)
- 1 cup (30 g) croutons
- 2 tablespoons (28 g) unsalted butter
- ⅓ cup (37 g) sliced almonds
- 1 pound (455 g) asparagus, trimmed
- 1 bunch broccolini, trimmed
- Ground black pepper, to taste
- 4 soft-boiled eggs, cooked for 1–2 minutes in the Instant Pot (page 115)
- ½ cup (112 g) crumbled feta cheese
- ¼ cup (23 g) thinly sliced Fresno chiles or ½ teaspoon crushed red pepper flakes

SERVES 4

Another nod to my beloved Southern California where we are never short on grilled vegetables, pesto, and runny eggs. This splendid combination gets even better when we add Mexican ingredients such as fresh cilantro, nutty pepitas, and fiery Fresno chiles. I love the bits of crunch from toasted bread crumbs and almonds, too. Don't worry—the bread crumbs are crushed up store-bought croutons that just need a buttery toss in the skillet to make them extra crispy.

❋ INSTRUCTIONS ❋

Heat a grill to medium heat (350° to 450°F [175° to 230°C]). Clean the grates and brush with oil. Combine the mint, cilantro, pepitas, garlic, and ½ teaspoon of salt in the bowl of a food processor fitted with the blade attachment. Blend on high while slowly adding 6 tablespoons (89 ml) of the oil. Turn off the food processor, scrape down the sides with a rubber spatula, and add the lemon juice. Blend once more until very smooth. Taste and add more salt, if needed. Scrape the pesto into a bowl, and wash and dry the food processor bowl and blade.

Add the croutons to the food processor. Pulse until they are coarse crumbs. Heat the butter in a medium frying pan over medium heat. Add the crouton crumbs and almonds and fry, stirring frequently, until lightly toasted and the almonds are golden brown.

Toss the asparagus and broccolini in the remaining oil, and season with salt and pepper. Grill with the lid closed until grill marks form and the vegetables are tender when pierced with a knife, about 10 minutes.

Arrange the asparagus and broccolini on a platter. Peel the eggs, cut in half, and nestle them in between the vegetables. Top with the pesto, the crouton-almond mixture, feta cheese, and Fresno chiles.

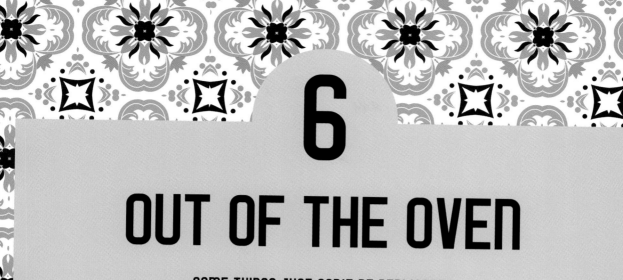

6
OUT OF THE OVEN

SOME THINGS JUST CAN'T BE REPLICATED.

The bubbly melted cheese of a pan of baked enchiladas, the flaky crust of a still-warm empanada, or the cozy warm feeling my midwestern heart gets at first sight of a blistered and browned casserole.

What do all these things have in common? They come straight out of the oven of course!

The appealing nature of the oven is you can put a dish in, walk away, and come back a little later to dinner. This fuss-free way of cooking is perfect for when you have a bit more time but don't want any more work. Whipping up a pan of veggies

baked in poblano cream sauce (page 160) or what my son calls the original nachos—Sheet-Pan Chilaquiles (page 163)—is extremely satisfying and requires very little cleanup.

These dishes also make excellent party food. Double or triple these recipes if you're serving more than just your immediate family. Add one of the salads from chapter 2 and a homemade salsa or two for the best way I know to "have people over."

ROASTED CARROT BARBACOA TOSTADAS WITH CHARRED JALAPEÑO YOGURT SAUCE

INGREDIENTS

FOR THE SAUCE

- 2 medium jalapeños
- 2 cloves garlic, unpeeled
- 1 cup (200 g) whole milk Greek yogurt
- 1 cup (16 g) fresh cilantro (tender leaves and stems)
- 2 tablespoons (30 ml) olive oil
- 1 tablespoon (15 ml) unseasoned rice vinegar
- 1 teaspoon kosher salt

FOR THE CARROTS

- 6 dried guajillo chiles, stemmed, seeded, and rinsed
- 1 bottle (12 ounces, or 355 ml) beer
- 1 small red onion, chopped
- ½ cup (8 g) fresh cilantro (tender leaves and stems)
- ½ cup (32 g) loosely packed fresh Mexican oregano or Mediterranean oregano, tough stems removed
- 6 cloves garlic
- ¼ cup (80 g) blackstrap molasses
- 1 teaspoon kosher salt
- ½ teaspoon ground cumin
- ¼ teaspoon ground black pepper
- 3 pounds (1.4 kg) carrots, trimmed, peeled, and cut in half

FOR THE TOSTADAS

- 1 cup (59 ml) avocado or sunflower oil
- 8 (6-inch, or 15-cm) corn tortillas
- A few pinches of kosher salt

SERVES 4

Sweet roasted carrots make excellent barbacoa. Traditional barbacoa involves slow roasted meat cooked in a wood-fired pit for hours and hours until it is tender and can be shredded into tacos. For a plant-based version roasted carrots are not authentic, but an extremely delicious alternative piled on a crispy-fried tostada with a creamy jalapeño yogurt sauce. This recipe calls for frying the tostadas. If you'd prefer to bake them, see page 80 or use store-bought tostadas.

❀ INSTRUCTIONS ❀

To make the sauce: Place the jalapeños and garlic in a dry comal or cast-iron skillet over medium-high heat. Cook until charred on all sides; the garlic will take less time so remove that first. Remove the garlic peel and the stems from the jalapeños. Cut the jalapeños in half and remove the seeds if you'd like it less spicy. Add the charred vegetables to a blender with the yogurt, cilantro, oil, vinegar, and salt. Blend on high until smooth. Taste and add more salt or vinegar as needed.

To make the carrots: Preheat the oven to 400°F (200°C, or gas mark 6). Bring a small saucepan of water to a boil. Add the guajillo chiles and remove from the heat. Let soak until tender, about 15 minutes. Drain the chiles and combine in a blender with the beer, onion, cilantro, oregano, garlic, molasses, salt, cumin, and black pepper.

Blend on high until smooth. Toss the carrots with the guajillo chile sauce in a large roasting pan until the carrots are well coated. Pour into a roasting pan and spread the carrots into an even layer. Roast until the carrots are tender and cooked through but not mushy, about 40 minutes.

Meanwhile, to make the tostadas: Heat the oil in a large frying pan over medium-high heat until shimmering. Add the tortillas one at a time and fry until crisp and golden, about 2 to 3 minutes. Drain on a paper towel–lined plate and sprinkle with a little salt. Pile the carrots on the tostada shells and drizzle with the jalapeño sauce.

Continued >

TECHNIQUE

●●●●●●●●●●●●●●●●●●●●●●●●●●●●●●

Frying a whole corn tortilla to make a tostada isn't a special skill, but if not done properly, can result in a tostada that is chewy and soggy instead of light and crisp—believe me, been there and have absolutely done that. The trick is to make sure your oil is hot when the tortilla goes in. To be absolutely sure, measure the temperature of your oil with a deep-fry thermometer (they are inexpensive and available online and in most grocery stores). It should be between 350° and 375°F (175° and 190°C). If you don't have a thermometer, stick the edge of the tortilla into the hot oil, and it should be immediately covered with bubbles. If not, wait another minute and try again.

SWEET PEA AND POTATO EMPANADAS WITH TAMARIND-CHIPOTLE DIPPING SAUCE

These empanadas are a bit more labor intensive than most recipes in this book, but they are so worth it. They are a mash-up of Indian samosas and Mexican empanadas. The ingredient similarities between these two cuisines have always been so fascinating to me. Cilantro, tamarind, chiles, lime, cumin, coriander, the list of ingredients loved by both cultures goes on and on even though they are a world apart. If you'd rather not make the tamarind sauce, the tomatillo-avocado salsa (page 73) would be equally good.

Continued >

INGREDIENTS

FOR THE DOUGH

- 1½ cups (188 g) all-purpose flour
- 1 teaspoon kosher salt
- ½ teaspoon granulated sugar
- 12 tablespoons (¾ cup [168 g]) cold, cubed unsalted butter or vegan butter
- ¼ cup (60 ml) ice water
- 1 large egg

FOR THE FILLING

- 8 ounces (225 g) russet potatoes, peeled, cut into ½-inch (2.5-cm) cubes
- ½ teaspoon kosher salt, plus more to taste
- 2 tablespoons (30 ml) avocado or sunflower oil
- ½ medium yellow onion, minced
- 1 medium serrano chile, seeded and minced
- 2 cloves garlic, minced
- 1 teaspoon ground coriander
- 1 teaspoon ground cumin
- ¼ teaspoon freshly ground black pepper
- ¼ cup (33 g) fresh or frozen peas
- 2 teaspoons (10 ml) fresh lime juice (from 1 lime)

FOR THE TAMARIND SAUCE

- 2 cups (475 ml) water
- ½ cup (115 g) packed brown sugar
- ¼ cup (63 g) tamarind pulp
- 1 teaspoon ground cumin
- 1 chipotle in adobo sauce, minced
- ½ teaspoon kosher salt
- ½ teaspoon paprika

SERVES 4

❊ INSTRUCTIONS ❊

To make the dough: Combine the flour, salt, and sugar in a large bowl. Add the butter and toss to coat in the flour. Using a pastry cutter, cut the butter into the flour until it is in small pea-sized pieces.

Drizzle ice water over the bowl and mix it in by scooping the flour up from the bottom and let the flour and water mix by falling through your fingers. It sounds weird, but you'll get the hang of it. Keep mixing in this motion until a clump of dough holds together when squeezed.

Gather the dough and form it into a ball. Wrap in plastic wrap and press down into a disk. Refrigerate the dough for at least 1 hour or overnight. The dough can also be made and frozen for up to 3 months.

To make the filling: Add the potatoes to a small saucepan and cover with water. Add a large pinch of salt and bring to a boil over high heat. Boil until just tender when poked with a sharp knife. Drain. Heat the oil in a large frying pan over medium-high heat. Add the onion, chiles, and garlic. Cook, stirring often for 3 minutes, until starting to soften and turn golden. Add the coriander, cumin, salt, and black pepper, and cook for 2 minutes to toast the spices. Stir in the potatoes, peas, and lime juice. Mix, mashing the potatoes slightly. Remove from the heat and set aside to cool.

To make the sauce: Combine the water, brown sugar, and tamarind in a small saucepan. Bring to a boil over medium heat and cook, stirring occasionally, until the sugar is dissolved and the tamarind is soft, about 10 minutes. Strain the mixture through a fine-mesh sieve into a heatproof bowl, pressing on the solids to extract as much of the liquid as possible. Return the liquid to the saucepan and add the remaining ingredients. Return to a boil and cook for 5 to 10 minutes, or until thickened slightly. Set aside until cool.

Preheat the oven to 375°F (190°C, or gas mark 5). Line two baking sheets with parchment paper.

Remove the dough from the refrigerator and place it on a lightly floured surface. Roll out to about ¼ inch (6 mm) thickness and cut into circles using a 4-inch (10-cm) round biscuit cutter. Gather the scraps, form into a ball, and re-roll the scraps until all the dough is used; you should have around 16 circles of dough.

TECHNIQUE

●●●●●●●●●●●●●●●●●●●●●●●●●●●●●●●●●●●●●●●

If you can't find tamarind paste, use 4 whole tamarind pods instead. Remove the papery outer skin, then cook the pods with the other ingredients as instructed. Once softened and the sugar is dissolved, let it cool a little bit. Pour the mixture in the blender and blend until liquefied. Warning: There are seeds inside the pods that will produce a very loud noise while blending. It's okay—it won't break your blender. Strain out the seeds and let the sauce cool.

Place about a tablespoon of filling on one half of the circle and fold the other half over to close, creating a half-moon shape. Press the two edges together to seal and use a small spoon to create a decorative edge, if desired. Beat the egg with a tablespoon (15 ml) of water.

Place the empanadas on the baking sheets, and using a pastry brush, brush the tops with the egg mixture. Bake the empanadas until they are golden brown and crisp on the bottom, about 25 to 30 minutes. Serve immediately with the tamarind sauce.

CLASSIC BEAN AND CHEESE MOLLETES WITH PICO DE GALLO

INGREDIENTS

- 1 long baguette, sliced in half
- ¼ cup (55 g) unsalted butter, softened
- A pinch of kosher salt and pepper
- 1 cup (230 g) Refried Beans (page 99)
- 1 cup (120 g) shredded sharp Cheddar cheese
- 1 cup (250 g) pico de gallo (page 137)
- ⅓ cup (77 g) Mexican crema (page 23)

SERVES 4

If you've never had the pleasure of enjoying a mollete, you have missed out on one of life's finest, simplest pleasures. This broiled, open-faced sandwich starts with a buttered baguette and ends with a spoonful of fresh pico de gallo on top. In the middle goes creamy refried beans and melty cheese. My favorite is a sharp, aged Cheddar, but queso Oaxaca (page 23) is more authentic.

Use one long crusty baguette and cut it into pieces, or Mexican bolillo rolls to make individual molletes, or take a cue from Mexican chef Gabriela Cámara and make them on a sweet concha roll sliced in half.

❋ INSTRUCTIONS ❋

Preheat the oven to 350°F (175°C, or gas mark 4). Slice a whole baguette into four pieces and then cut each piece in half horizontally. Spread with butter, and sprinkle with salt and pepper. Place the bread on a foil or parchment-lined baking sheet and toast until the edges are golden brown with soft centers, about 8 to 10 minutes. Remove the bread from the oven and turn the broiler to high.

Divide the refried beans evenly between the bread pieces and spread to the edges. Top with cheese and place under the broiler. Toast until the cheese is melted, golden brown, and bubbling, about 3 minutes. Top with pico de gallo and a drizzle of crema.

WEEKNIGHT CHEESY ENCHILADAS WITH HOMEMADE ENCHILADA SAUCE

INGREDIENTS

- 1 recipe Enchilada Sauce (page 111) or your favorite store-bought enchilada sauce
- 16 (6-inch, or 15-cm) corn tortillas
- 4 cups (400 g) shredded cheese (mozzarella, Monterey jack, pepper jack, Cheddar, or a mixture of these)

SERVES 4

This recipe is to prove that you can make a pan of decadent, cheesy enchiladas from start to finish in under an hour on any weeknight. There are three ingredients (well the homemade enchilada sauce has its own set of ingredients, but it's pretty minimal too). Point is, you can do this! These are not enchiladas as you would find them in Mexico—if you're craving that, try the enmoladas (page 71). These are the enchiladas that you would find in my husband's home state of Texas: super cheesy, bubbly, and baked to perfection.

❋ INSTRUCTIONS ❋

Preheat the oven to 375°F (190°C, or gas mark 5). Grease a 9- x 13-inch (23- x 33-cm) baking dish. Spread ½ cup (120 ml) of the enchilada sauce on the bottom of the baking dish.

Heat a comal or cast-iron skillet over medium heat for at least 3 minutes, or until hot but not smoking. Warm the tortillas on the comal until soft and pliable but not toasted. Keep warm by wrapping them in a clean kitchen towel or tortilla warmer.

Fill each tortilla with 2 tablespoons (about 13 g) of the cheese. Roll to close and lay them in the prepared baking dish seam-side down. Repeat with the remaining tortillas and cheese. Cover the enchiladas with the sauce, then top with the remaining cheese.

Bake until the sauce is bubbling, and the cheese is melted and browned in spots, about 15 minutes.

ONE-PAN CHEESY RICE CHILE RELLENO CASSEROLE

INGREDIENTS

- 6 large poblano chiles
- ¼ cup (55 g) butter
- 1 large white onion, chopped
- 3 cloves garlic
- 1½ cups (278 g) jasmine rice
- 4 large tomatoes, chopped
- 1 teaspoon dried oregano
- 1 pound (455 g) Oaxaca cheese, cubed
- 3 cups (705 ml) water
- 1 teaspoon kosher salt, plus more to taste
- Ground black pepper, to taste

SERVES 4 TO 6

The summer I grew poblano chiles in my garden for the first time, I got a little plant from my local nursery and put it in a small, sunny spot. I thought it would get to be the same 2-foot size as the other pepper plants I have grown in the past. A month later, this little plant had taken over the entire bed, staked in what seemed like a million places to keep it from crushing everything in sight. This gorgeous giant kept us well stocked with poblano chiles all year long and the ones we didn't get to eat fresh got dried and turned into ancho chiles (which is what they are called when dried).

This cheesy rice casserole was a particular favorite during our poblano bounty. The grassy peppers are the ones used to make chile rellenos, the traditional cheese-stuffed peppers that are fried and served with a silky tomato sauce. I've captured all those flavors in this easy-to-make baked dish reminiscent of ones my grandma would make when I was growing up—which means I'm one step closer to fulfilling my lifelong goal of becoming my grandmother.

❊ INSTRUCTIONS ❊

Preheat the oven to 425°F (220°C, or gas mark 7). Char the poblanos over a gas flame or under the broiler. Turn every couple of minutes to evenly char on all sides. Place in a heatproof bowl and cover with plastic wrap. Let sit until cool enough to handle. Peel off the charred skin and rinse under cold water. Remove the stems and seeds, and chop in large pieces.

Heat the butter in a small 4-6 quart, oven-safe Dutch oven with a lid over medium heat. Once the butter is melted and foaming, add the onion and garlic. Season with salt and pepper. Cook until tender. Add the rice and stir frequently, until the rice is opaque and golden. Add the poblanos, tomatoes, oregano, Oaxaca cheese, water, and salt. Stir to combine. Cover and bake until the rice is cooked, about 30 minutes. Uncover and bake 10 minutes more, or until the top is golden and bubbly.

POWER-UP YOUR VEGGIES

•••

Poblano chile peppers are ubiquitous in Mexican cooking. The smell of a poblano charring over an open flame has the power to drop you into the heart of Mexico without ever leaving your kitchen. They are also good for you, high in antioxidants and vitamins A and C. Eat more poblanos! They can be grilled, sautéed, stuffed, roasted, but the most common way to enjoy them is to char the skins until they are blackened, then peel the charred skin off, remove the stems and seeds, and slice them into thin strips.

BAKED SWEET POTATO FLAUTAS WITH VEGAN QUESO

INGREDIENTS

FOR THE FLAUTAS

- 1–1½ pounds (680 g) sweet potato (1 large or 2 small)
- 1 tablespoon (15 g) plus ½ teaspoon kosher salt, divided
- 1 tablespoon (15 ml) lime juice (from 1 lime)
- 12 (6-inch, or 15-cm) corn tortillas
- 2 tablespoons (30 ml) avocado oil

FOR THE VEGAN QUESO

- 2 tablespoons (30 ml) avocado oil
- ¾ cup (103 g) raw cashews
- ¾ cup (175 ml) hot water
- 2 tablespoons (30 ml) fresh lime juice (from 1 lime)
- 1 can (4 ounces, or 115 g) diced green chiles, juice and all
- ¼ cup (20 g) nutritional yeast
- ½ teaspoon smoked paprika
- 2½ teaspoons (13 g) kosher salt

SERVES 4

It is not in my nature to do something so unorthodox as bake a flauta or create a vegan queso, but as an infinitely curious cook I was willing to give it a try. For you. My first attempts were less than stellar: hard tortillas, gritty queso, chewiness where there shouldn't have been any . . . but by test twelve, I was on to something! The key to getting crispy flautas (or taquitos as some people call them) is to warm the tortillas before filling; a hot, hot oven; and brushing them with a good amount of oil before they go in. As for the vegan queso, frying the cashews until they are a dark golden brown is the way to get that unmistakable queso umami.

❋ INSTRUCTIONS ❋

To make the flautas: Preheat the oven to 450°F (230°C, or gas mark 8). Place an oven rack in the top of the oven. Peel the sweet potato, cut into ½-inch (1-cm)-thick pieces, and place them in a small saucepan. Fill the pan with water about three-quarters of the way and add a tablespoon (15 g) of salt. Bring to a boil over medium-high heat. Reduce the heat to a simmer and cook until the sweet potatoes are tender, but not falling apart.

Drain and let sit in the colander for a few minutes to dry. Return to the saucepan with the ½ teaspoon of salt and the lime juice. Mash really well with a potato masher until smooth.

Heat a comal or cast-iron skillet over medium heat for at least 3 minutes, or until hot but not smoking. Warm the tortillas one at a time on the comal until soft and pliable, but not toasted. Keep warm in a clean kitchen towel or in a tortilla warmer.

Place about 2 tablespoons (xx g) of the sweet potato filling on one edge of each tortilla and roll up to close.

Grease a baking sheet with cooking spray. Lay the flautas, seam-side down, on the baking sheet and generously brush the tops with the avocado oil. Use all the oil. Bake until crispy and toasted, about 20 minutes. Serve hot with the queso dip.

To make the queso: Heat the oil in a large frying pan over medium heat. Add the cashews and fry, stirring occasionally, until the nuts are really toasted. Transfer to a blender with the remaining ingredients and blend until smooth. Return to the frying pan and heat until just warm.

VEGGIES BAKED IN CREAMY ROASTED POBLANO SAUCE

My husband Armando's Tía Irma was a fabulous cook. I can't tell you how often he has told me about this chicken dish she used to make with a creamy green sauce. He can't tell me what was in it, or how she made it, but he does remember that it was dreamy eyes amazing. Sadly, I can't consult with her as she passed away a few years ago. Instead, I've asked all the Mexican cooks I know and done hours of internet and cookbook research, and while he's convinced she made it on the stove, this oven-baked version is pretty darn close. Of course, we are leaving out the chicken here and instead swapping in a hearty mixture of baby red potatoes, sweet carrots, broccoli, and cauliflower for a cozy winter dish. Serve with the Oven-Baked Garlic-Cilantro Rice (page 175) to soak up all the delicious poblano sauce.

Continued >

INGREDIENTS

- 4 poblano chiles
- 1 large white onion, quartered
- 6 cloves garlic, peeled
- 1 container (16 ounces, or 455 g) Mexican crema (page 23)
- 2 teaspoons (10 g) kosher salt
- 1 pound (455 g) red baby potatoes, cut in half
- 1 pound (455 g) carrots, cut in 2-inch (5-cm) pieces, large pieces cut in half
- 1 small head cauliflower, cut into large florets
- 1 small head broccoli, cut into large florets
- 1 (6-ounce, or 168-g) package baby spinach
- 5 ounces (140 g) Cotija cheese, crumbled

SERVES 4 TO 6

❀ INSTRUCTIONS ❀

Heat the broiler to high, and arrange the rack to the top of the oven. Place the poblanos, onion, and garlic on a baking sheet. Char the vegetables under the broiler, turning frequently so they are evenly blackened on all sides. Remove the garlic when it is golden brown; it will be ready before the poblanos and onion.

Once the vegetables are charred, remove them from the oven and set the oven to bake at 400°F (200°C, or gas mark 6).

Transfer the onions and garlic to a blender. Place the poblano chiles in a bowl and cover with plastic wrap until cool enough to handle. Once cool, rub off the charred skin, remove the stem and seeds, and run under cold water to remove any excess skin or seeds. Place in the blender with the onions and garlic. Add the Mexican crema and salt. Blend on high until smooth.

Bring a large pot of heavily salted water to a boil over high heat. Add the baby potatoes and cook until just tender on the outside but still really firm on the inside when you poke one half with a sharp knife, about 8 minutes. Remove with a slotted spoon to a large bowl.

Return the water to a boil and add the carrots. Cook until they are the same as the potatoes, a little tender on the outside but still very firm on the inside, about 7 minutes. Remove with a slotted spoon to the large bowl with the potatoes.

Now blanch the cauliflower and broccoli in the same way, plunging into the boiling water and cooking until just barely tender, about 4 minutes. Remove with a slotted spoon to the large bowl with the potatoes. Add the baby spinach and pour the poblano sauce over the vegetables. Toss to completely coat the vegetables in the sauce.

Butter a 9- x 13-inch baking dish (23- x 33-cm) and transfer the vegetables and all the sauce to the baking dish. Sprinkle with the Cotija cheese. Bake until bubbly, about 30 minutes.

TECHNIQUE

●●●●●●●●●●●●●●●●●●●●●●●●●●●●●●

Blanching vegetables is a tried-and-true technique used in restaurant kitchens, often to prep them for other uses. If you have veggies that you don't know what to do with, cut them into bite-sized pieces, dunk them into boiling salted water, and cook until just barely tender. Drain them and immediately cover with ice water to preserve their color and stop the cooking. Once they are cool, drain and eat them with a drizzle of olive oil and a sprinkling of salt, or sauté them with garlic, or bake like in this dish. Or cover and keep them in the refrigerator for up to three days.

SHEET-PAN CHILAQUILES WITH LIME CREMA

INGREDIENTS

FOR THE SAUCE

- 3 dried ancho chiles, stemmed, seeded, and rinsed
- 2 medium tomatoes, cored
- ½ medium white onion, cut in half
- 2 medium jalapeños, stemmed and seeds removed if you like it less spicy
- 1 cup (16 g) chopped fresh cilantro (tender leaves and stems)
- 2 teaspoons (10 g) kosher salt
- 2 tablespoons (28 ml) lime juice (from 1 lime)
- 1 bag (12 ounces, or 340 g) tortilla chips
- 2 cups (344 g) cooked pinto beans
- 2 cups (264 g) crumbled queso fresco

FOR SERVING

- ¼ large white onion, minced
- ½ cup (8 g) chopped fresh cilantro (tender leaves and stems)
- 1 cup (115 g) radishes, thinly sliced
- 1 recipe Lime Crema (page 85)

SERVES 4

Okay, so chilaquiles are not only responsible for my love affair with Mexican food, but also are the best way to use up stale tortillas, salsa, the quarter of an onion I inevitably have in my fridge, and the bunch of cilantro wilting away on my counter. In other words, it's my savior.

Typically, chilaquiles is a breakfast dish made by frying last night's tortillas with salsa and topping with an egg or two, but since my fondest memories are of eating it late at night under the fluorescent glow of the restaurant kitchen after the dinner rush was over, I think of it as dinner.

This version hangs on the coattails of the sheet-pan craze mainly because it means I have to wash one less pan and the amount of oil splattered on my kitchen floor is greatly reduced. Sometimes I care, sometimes I don't. Anyhoo, it's an easier way to make chilaquiles. If you want to make it even easier, skip making the salsa and use leftover Instant Pot Mole Amarillo (page 100) or your favorite store-bought salsa. This is also an excellent occasion to use any leftover homemade tortilla chips (page 167) you may have around.

❊ INSTRUCTIONS ❊

To make the sauce: Bring a small saucepan of water to a boil over high heat.

Heat a comal or cast-iron skillet over medium heat for at least 3 minutes, or until hot but not smoking. Place the dried chiles, tomatoes, onion, and jalapeños on the comal and toast, until the chiles and vegetables are browned and beginning to char on all sides. Keep turning and flipping each piece and removing them from the pan as they brown. Transfer the ancho chiles to the pan of boiling water and remove from the heat. Submerge the chiles and let soak until soft and pliable, at least 10 minutes.

Transfer the remaining vegetables to a blender. Remove the soaked chiles with tongs and save the soaking liquid. Add them to the blender along with the cilantro, salt, lime juice, and 1 cup (235 ml) of the soaking liquid. Blend until smooth.

Preheat the oven to 350°F (175°C, or gas mark 4) and arrange the rack to the top of the oven. Line a baking sheet with foil or parchment paper. Combine the chips and salsa in a large bowl. Toss until the chips are well coated in sauce, being careful not to break the chips too much. Spread in an even layer on the prepared baking sheet. Top with the pinto beans and queso fresco. Cook in the oven until hot and cheese is melted, about 15 minutes. Turn broiler to high and broil until browned, about 3 minutes.

To serve: Garnish with the onion, cilantro, radishes, and crema.

7
EXTRAS

MY INTENTION FOR THIS BOOK IS THAT YOU CAN PICK ALMOST ANY RECIPE IN THE PREVIOUS CHAPTERS AND CALL IT DINNER.

With a few exceptions, like the Instant Pot Mole Amarillo on page 100, they were made to be satisfying all on their own, with perhaps a side of warm tortillas or some chips.

There are those occasions, however, when you may want more . . . that's where these recipes come in! These recipes round out a meal nicely and are all quick and simple to make. Maybe

you're having people over and want something to snack on ahead of the main dish. Or maybe you're just hungry! Whatever the reason, you'll find plenty of ideas on the pages that follow.

HOMEMADE TORTILLA CHIPS WITH FLAVORED SALTS

INGREDIENTS

- 2 cups (472 ml) avocado or sunflower oil
- 10–12 (6-inch, or 15-cm) corn tortillas, cut like a pizza into 8 wedges
- 1–2 teaspoons kosher salt or flavored salt (below) for sprinkling

SERVES 4

● ● ● ● ● ● ● ● ● ● ● ● ● ● ● ●

Do you want to know the secret to world peace? Homemade tortilla chips. Really, if the world knew how easy it was to make tortilla chips, I think it would at least be a happier place. This philosophy could be why no one has asked me to be a UN ambassador, yet it could be the answer for your happy home like it is for mine.

Crisp tortilla chips, or *totopos*, still warm from the pan and sprinkled with salt, are so much better than anything you can buy in a bag—and they take little effort. Get fancy and sprinkle them with a flavored salt, or kosher salt is good too!

❀ INSTRUCTIONS ❀

Heat the oil in a large frying pan to 350°F (175°C), or until the edge of a tortilla is covered immediately with bubbles when submerged in the oil.

Add the tortilla wedges a handful at a time into the hot oil, spreading them out so they cover the entire pan and are not sticking together.

Fry until golden brown on both sides, turning occasionally with tongs or a bamboo skimmer, about 2 to 3 minutes. Transfer to a paper towel–lined plate, and sprinkle with salt while still warm.

FLAVORED SALTS

● ● ● ● ● ● ● ● ● ● ● ● ● ● ● ● ●

These make enough for several batches of chips. Any leftover can be stored in a sealed container at room temperature for up to 6 months. They are great for rimming margarita glasses too!

Habanero Salt
Combine ½ cup (120 g) of kosher salt with ½ teaspoon habanero chile powder. Stir with a spoon to combine. Sprinkle on a chip and see if it is spicy enough. If you'd like more heat, add ¼ teaspoon more chile powder.

Jamaica Salt
In a molcajete (page 29) or clean coffee grinder, grind ¼ cup (10 g) jamaica (dried hibiscus flowers, page 27) with 1 tablespoon (15 g) of kosher salt to a fine powder. Stir with ½ cup (120 g) of salt until evenly combined.

Tequila Salt
Stir together 2 tablespoons (28 ml) of blanco tequila and ½ cup (120 g) kosher salt in a bowl until all the salt is evenly wet. Spread the salt on a large plate in an even layer and let dry overnight on the counter. Once the salt is completely dry, it is ready to use.

SUNDAY SALSITA

INGREDIENTS

- ¼ cup (59 ml) olive oil
- 2 medium jalapeños, stemmed and chopped
- 1 medium white onion, diced
- 2 large tomatoes, diced
- 3 cloves garlic, chopped
- 1 teaspoon kosher salt

SERVES 4

I cannot take credit for this recipe: this is my husband's invention. It's a recipe he makes frequently on Sunday mornings to go with scrambled eggs, tortillas, and refried beans. It is warm in temperature and spice level, and an obvious choice for any time you want something quick and spicy to spoon over your meal.

❀ INSTRUCTIONS ❀

Heat the oil in a large frying pan over medium heat. Once it's shimmering, add the jalapeños, onion, tomatoes, garlic, and salt.

Cook, stirring frequently, until the vegetables are very soft and caramelized, about 10 minutes.

ROASTED KABOCHA SQUASH

INGREDIENTS

- 3 pounds (1.4 kg) kabocha squash, peeled and seeded
- 1 tablespoon (15 ml) olive oil
- 1 teaspoon ground cumin
- 1 teaspoon kosher salt
- ½ teaspoon ground coriander
- ¼ teaspoon ground cinnamon

SERVES 4

● ● ● ● ● ● ● ● ● ● ● ● ● ● ●

This recipe is for kabocha squash, but the spice mix and technique can be used for any squash or even sweet potatoes. Still, I'm a big fan of kabocha squash for its dense texture and nutty, sweet, intense flavor. It is also fairly easy to peel, something that can't be said for some other squashes (like acorn squash). This squash is amazing covered in Instant Pot Mole Amarillo (page 100).

❇ INSTRUCTIONS ❇

Preheat the oven to 425°F (220°C, or gas mark 7).

Cut the squash into 6 to 8 large wedges. Lay it on a baking sheet and drizzle with the oil, rubbing the oil all over the wedges.

Mix the spices together in a small bowl, then sprinkle them all over the squash. Toss the squash to coat the pieces with the spice mixture. Roast until a fork easily slips into the squash pieces, about 45 minutes.

TECHNIQUE

● ●

Cutting and peeling a rock hard kabocha squash can be challenging. The easiest way to do it is to slice off both ends with a very sharp chef's knife. Lay the squash cut-side down on the cutting board so it doesn't wobble around and cut the squash in half. Scoop the seeds out with a large soup spoon, then peel each half with a Y-peeler, the inexpensive (but extraordinarily useful) vegetable peeler shaped like the letter Y. Peel the squash as many times as necessary to remove the skin. Cut into wedges and you're good to go!

CHILES AND SCALLIONS TOREADOS

INGREDIENTS

- 5 medium jalapeños
- 1 bunch scallions, trimmed
- ¼ cup (60 ml) soy sauce
- ¼ cup (60 ml) lime juice (from 2 limes)

SERVES 4

The history of Chinese influence in Mexican cuisine dates back nearly 450 years ago when Spanish traders brought Eastern goods to the western border of Mexico to be traded for silver. In places such as Sonora and the Baja Peninsula, soy sauce is as common as hot sauce. These Chiles and Scallions Toreados are one of the fascinating mash-up dishes that are completely and authentically Mexican. The soy-marinated vegetables are a popular side dish with carne asada and also go well with Grilled Cauliflower Tacos (page 126) and Sangria-Marinated Veggie Skewers (page 123).

❈ INSTRUCTIONS ❈

Roll the jalapeños on a counter, gently pressing down with the palm of your hand to release the seeds and intensify their heat. Heat a comal or cast-iron skillet over medium heat for at least 3 minutes, or until hot but not smoking. Place the jalapeños and scallions on the comal for about 10 minutes, flipping often, until blackened, wrinkled, and softened on all sides.

Transfer them to a medium bowl with the soy sauce and lime juice. Stir and let marinate at least 10 minutes.

POWER-UP YOUR VEGGIES

I write a blog called *¡Hola! Jalapeño* so you know my love of jalapeños is real. Named after the city of Xalapa (pronounced Ha-la-pa), Veracruz, Mexico, where the chile peppers are originally from, the use of the jalapeño for its nutritional and medicinal properties dates to the Aztecs. According to the American Heart Association, consumption of chile peppers, such as jalapeños, is associated with a 25 percent reduction in death from any cause! To easily remove their fiery seeds, slice off the stem, then make a cut lengthwise down the chile, avoiding the seeds or white membrane. Flip the jalapeño so it is cut-side down on the cutting board and continue making these vertical cuts around the chile until all you're left with is the oblong pocket of seeds that runs down the middle and four seedless strips of jalapeño.

OVEN-BAKED GARLIC-CILANTRO RICE

INGREDIENTS

- 2 tablespoons (30 ml) avocado oil
- ½ small white onion, chopped
- 3 cloves garlic, minced
- 1 cup (185 g) white jasmine rice
- ½ teaspoon kosher salt
- 1¾ cups (410 ml) vegetable broth
- ½ cup (8 g) chopped fresh cilantro (tender leaves and stems)

SERVES 4

We eat a lot of rice in my house. To break up the monotony of steamed white rice with every meal, I sometimes make this easy oven-baked version, perfumed with garlic and cilantro. This foolproof method of cooking rice may take a bit longer than doing it on the stove, but takes away any anxiety about burning the rice or worrying that the bottom half will be mushy and the top half still raw. If you have an oven-safe frying pan with a lid, you can make this all in one pan. If your frying pan doesn't have an oven-safe lid, use a piece of foil instead to cover it, or transfer everything to a baking dish and cover that with foil instead.

❀ INSTRUCTIONS ❀

Preheat the oven to 350°F (175°C, or gas mark 4). Heat the oil in a large frying pan over medium heat. Add the onion, garlic, rice, and salt. Cook until the onions are tender and translucent and the rice has gone from being shiny to opaque and browned in spots, about 5 minutes.

Add the broth and stir to combine. Cover and transfer to the oven. Bake until the rice is tender, about 30 minutes. Let stand, covered, 10 minutes. Add the cilantro, stir to combine, and serve immediately.

CHIPOTLE-GARLIC ROASTED KALE

INGREDIENTS

- 10 ounces (90 g) kale, tough stems removed and torn into bite-sized pieces
- 3 tablespoons (45 ml) olive oil
- 3 cloves garlic, minced
- ¼ teaspoon kosher salt
- ½ teaspoon chipotle chile flakes

SERVES 4

Roasting kale tenderizes it a bit but also crisps up the edges. Tossed with a simple spicy blend of smoky chipotle chile flakes and garlic makes it downright irresistible. This may seem like a slew of kale for just four people, but the kale cooks down to half its size and any leftovers keep great covered in the refrigerator for up to 5 days. To reheat, just quickly sauté with a bit of oil in a frying pan until warm.

Serve this Chipotle-Garlic Roasted Kale with the Fideo Seco on page 93 or on top of the sweet potatoes on page 117.

❀ INSTRUCTIONS ❀

Preheat the oven to 450°F (230°C, or gas mark 8) and arrange an oven rack in the top of the oven. Wash kale thoroughly and dry well. Place on a large baking sheet and drizzle with olive oil then sprinkle with garlic, salt, and chile flakes.

Massage the seasonings into the kale for a minute or so or until the leaves are well coated.

Roast on the top shelf for 10 minutes or until crisp on the edges but still supple and tender in the middle.

STEWED GREEN BEANS WITH TOMATOES AND MEXICAN OREGANO

INGREDIENTS

- 3 tablespoons (45 ml) olive oil
- 1 large white onion, medium dice
- 1 clove garlic, minced
- 1 teaspoon kosher salt
- A few pinches of ground black pepper
- 2 medium fresh tomatoes, chopped
- 2 teaspoons (2 g) dried Mexican oregano
- 1 cup (235 ml) water
- 1 pound (455 g) fresh green beans, trimmed and cut into 2-inch (5-cm) pieces
- 1 lemon, thinly sliced
- ½ cup (24 g) fresh basil leaves, torn into pieces if large

SERVES 4

This could easily serve as a summery side dish to the Marinated Vegetable Torta (page 55) or the Stuffed Poblanos (page 133), but I often serve this with the Mexican rice (page 115) instead of (or sometimes in addition to) the boiled eggs and avocado pico de gallo.

These well-cooked green beans are in contrast to how most people prefer their beans these days, but with their silky texture and rich tomato sauce I know you'll be hooked. I learned this recipe from my mother-in-law, who also uses the same method to cook nopales, the pads of the Opuntia cactus.

The lemon slices stirred in at the end are meant to add a faint lemony flavor and beautiful color, but I don't suggest eating them whole.

❋ INSTRUCTIONS ❋

Heat the oil in a large frying pan over medium-high heat. Add the onion, garlic, salt, and black pepper. Cook for 5 to 6 minutes, until translucent and just starting to brown.

Add the tomatoes, oregano, water, and green beans. Bring to a boil, and reduce the heat to a simmer. Cover and cook for 20 minutes, or until the beans are soft and dark green (but aren't falling apart) and the tomatoes have cooked down into a thick sauce. Taste and add more salt and pepper, if necessary. Stir in the lemon slices and basil leaves.

CILANTRO-LIME SLAW

INGREDIENTS

- ¼ medium head red cabbage, thinly sliced
- ¼ medium head green cabbage, thinly sliced
- 1 large carrot, julienned or grated
- ¼ small red onion, thinly sliced
- ¼ cup (4 g) chopped fresh cilantro (tender leaves and stems)
- 2 tablespoons (28 ml) lime juice (from 1 lime), plus more to taste
- 1 tablespoon (15 ml) avocado oil
- ½ teaspoon kosher salt, plus more to taste

SERVES 4

● ● ● ● ● ● ● ● ● ● ● ● ● ● ● ● ● ●

For me, there is always room on the table for this bright cabbage slaw. Honestly, I make it at least twice a week. It is super crunchy, goes with everything, and I can make it up to an hour in advance and it is more than happy to patiently wait (and even improves) while I make the rest of our dinner. We eat it with tacos, tostadas, enchiladas, and it tops our bowls of rice and beans, tortilla soup (page 107), and pozole. I can't think of anything in this book it wouldn't be good with.

❀ INSTRUCTIONS ❀

Add the vegetables and cilantro to a large bowl and toss to combine. Drizzle the lime juice and oil over the vegetables, and sprinkle with salt. Toss everything together until the vegetables are well coated. Taste and season with more salt or lime juice, if needed.

TECHNIQUE

● ●

I've said it before, and I'll say it again, I'm not big on kitchen gadgets— but one tool I turn to again and again is my Japanese mandoline. This simple, inexpensive piece of equipment makes even, thin slices a snap and is essential for making this slaw in minutes. Running the cabbage through the mandoline doesn't really need an explanation but you can cut the carrot on it, too. Make thin slices of the whole carrot with the mandoline, then stack the slices on each other and use a sharp chef's knife to cut them into long julienne strips. Don't know what else to use it for? How about thinly slicing the radishes for the Aguachile (page 51) or the garlic cloves to make the Guajillo Chile Garlic Oil (page 102).

AGUA DE JAMAICA

INGREDIENTS

- ½ cup (20 g) jamaica (dried hibiscus flowers, page 27), rinsed with cold water
- 3 cups (705 ml) water
- ½ cup (100 g) granulated sugar
- 1 lime, cut into wedges

SERVES 4

This being the only drink recipe in this book should signify how special and deserving it is of that honor. I'm not only including it because it would pain me greatly if you made the jamaica filling (page 65) and then threw the sacred liquid down the drain, but also because agua de jamaica is, in my opinion, the queen of aguas frescas (those thirst-quenching juices Mexico is famous for). It goes with everything in this book and is loved by kids and adults alike (especially when a splash of tequila is added in the mix). It makes sensational paletas with chopped ripe mango, and it can even be cooked down into an excellent syrup.

❀ INSTRUCTIONS ❀

Combine the jamaica flowers, water, and sugar in a large saucepan. Bring to a boil over medium-high heat. Reduce the heat to a simmer and stir until the sugar is dissolved. Remove from the heat and let steep 10 minutes.

Strain, and reserve the jamaica flowers to use in the sopes filling (page 65). Let the agua de jamaica cool, and serve over ice with a lime wedge.

If you're making the recipe on page 65, here's how to make agua de jamaica with the soaking liquid.

INGREDIENTS

- 3 cups (705 ml) leftover soaking liquid from the jamaica filling on page 65
- ½ cup (100 g) granulated sugar
- 1 lime, cut into wedges

Combine the liquid and sugar in a large saucepan. Bring to a boil over medium-high heat. Reduce the heat to a simmer and cook for 10 minutes, stirring frequently, until all the sugar is dissolved. Remove from the heat and let cool. Serve over ice with a lime wedge.

HOW TO DOCTOR A CAN OF BEANS

INGREDIENTS

- 2 tablespoons (30 ml) olive oil
- 1 yellow onion, chopped
- 2 small jalapeños, chopped (seeds removed if you'd like it less spicy)
- A few pinches of kosher salt and black pepper
- 3 cloves garlic, minced
- 1½ teaspoons ground cumin
- 2 teaspoons (4 g) ancho chile powder
- 1 teaspoon ground coriander
- 1 teaspoon dried Mexican oregano
- 1 can (15 ounces, or 425 g) black, pinto, or cannellini beans

SERVES 4

Even though I've already told you how easy and fast it is to make dried beans in your electric cooker, there may be times when you just want to pop open a can of beans and call it done. There's no shame in that (I do it all the time), but you still want those beans to taste good.

Let me ask you this: Do you drain that can of beans before heating them up? Well, stop it! Unless you are mixing them into a salad or using them as a filling, don't get rid of the liquid in the can. It's got flavor, man! Why are you dumping it down the drain? Let's use it and add a little sofrito to those beans while we're at it.

❁ INSTRUCTIONS ❁

Heat the oil in a medium pan over medium-high heat. Add the onion and jalapeños, and season with salt and pepper. Let cook, stirring occasionally, until starting to brown.

Add the garlic, cumin, chile powder, coriander, and oregano. Cook, stirring to toast the spices for 1 minute. Add the beans, juice and all, and bring to a simmer. Simmer for about 5 minutes. Mash a bit with a potato masher to make them nice and creamy. You don't want to make a puree, just break some up to thicken the beans.

INSPIRATIONS

Not being Mexican myself, I've leaned hard on a lot of people to teach me everything I know about Mexican cooking.

I am forever grateful for the open hearts of my coworkers at Mustards Grill and beyond who first showed me the beauty that is Mexican food. Of course, after meeting my husband, Armando, I relied heavily on his aunts and mother to teach me those special recipes he grew up eating so I could then pass them along to our children

From there, I've devoured Mexican cookbooks, studied what innovative Mexican chefs such as Enrique Olvera, Javier Plascencia, and Sheyla Alvarado are up to and been inspired by other food bloggers who are doing incredible work creating their own special versions of Mexican cuisine.

What follows is a partial list of those who inspire and influence my work on a daily basis.

A Few of My Favorite Cookbooks

Pati's Mexican Table: The Secrets of Real Mexican Home Cooking by Pati Jinich

Pati Jinich is best known for her PBS cooking show where she travels around her native Mexico and discovers true treasures of Mexican cooking. Her first cookbook is one I turn to often. The recipes are interesting, unique, and innovative. I've never made one that I didn't absolutely love.

The Baja California Cookbook: Exploring the Good Life in Mexico by David Castro Hussong and Jay Porter

What a joy this book is, especially if you've experienced northern Baja firsthand. David Castro Hussong's family goes back generations in this part of Mexico and the history alone makes this book a good read but his recipes really capture the spirit of this very special place.

Nopalito: A Mexican Kitchen by Gonzalo Guzmán and Stacy Adimando

There are a lot of books written by chefs whose recipes don't come close to what you'd actually get at their restaurants but Nopalito is different. The easy-to-execute recipes taste exactly like the ones I've enjoyed many times at chef Guzmán's popular San Francisco restaurant—in other words, they're killer!

My Mexico City Kitchen: Recipes and Convictions by Gabriela Cámara and Malena Watrous

Fresh. This is the word that pops into my head whenever I think about this cookbook. Cámara's recipes are bright and airy. They offer a completely different perspective on Mexican cooking that I turn to when I'm looking for a lighter touch but one that is still deeply rooted in Mexican food traditions.

Mexican Food Bloggers I Love

As a food blogger myself, I am in constant contact with my fellow bloggers whether that's scrolling through their images on Instagram or checking in with their websites to see their latest recipes. They are my most intimate source of inspiration because I consider them dear friends who have been compassionate and generous with their time and expertise. I can't urge you enough to check out their sites if you aren't already.

Karla Zazueta

mexicanfoodmemories.co.uk

Karla writes *Mexican Food Memories* from her home in London, England. Born and raised in Ensenada, Mexico, Karla has a unique knack to make everything mouthwatering. She shares the foods she remembers having in her parents' home in Mexico and you can feel that love through her recipes and images.

Continued >

Susana Villasuso

www.lifelimonysal.com

Susana is also a Mexican expat living in London and her love of Mexican food just pours through her gorgeous images and modern recipes. Her site, *Life, Limon y Sal* is so beautiful and full of passionate but simple recipes I want to make for my family.

Alejandra Graf

www.brownsugarandvanilla.com

Alejandra grew up in Mexico, but now lives in Houston and blogs about vegan food, many with Mexican flavors and much more! Her site, *Brown Sugar and Vanilla*, is where I go when I want delicious, approachable vegan recipes that I know will please everyone around my table.

RESOURCES

Like most people these days, if I can't find what I'm looking for at my local Latin market, I buy it from a big online retailer. That said, there is an ever-growing number of small businesses selling Mexican goods and ingredients. Here are a few of my favorites:

Artelexia

artelexia.com

This shop lives up to its name as "The BEST Mexican Gift Shop"! Based in San Diego, California, Artelexia has everything from Mexican cookbooks to kitchen tools and more. Owner Elexia de la Parra sources much of what you find in the shop straight from Mexico, and you'll always find something unique and special whether shopping in-store or online. Many of the glassware, linens, and dishes used in the images in this book are from Artelexia.

Lola's Mercadito

www.etsy.com/shop/LolasMercadito

Lola Dweck is my go-to source for salsas, jams, tableware, and more. Her online shop is full of gourmet and artisan goods, some of which she makes herself—like her incredible Hibiscus Jam and salsas— and some come from makers in Mexico.

Yoli Tortilleria

www.eatyoli.com

As a midwestern girl I feel all kinds of joy that handmade tortillas are being made in Kansas City. They make non-GMO stone-ground corn tortillas and Sonoran-style flour tortillas that can be bought in their store or online.

Masienda

masienda.com/shop

Masienda partners with hundreds of traditional farmers to sell single-origin ingredients such as heirloom corn, beans, tortillas, masa harina, and more. Their tortillas are sold in many Whole Foods Markets across the country and their online store has these food items as well as molinos, tortilla presses, and tableware.

La Newyorkina

www.lanewyorkina.com

If you are lucky enough to live in New York, you may have visited Fany Gerson's Mexican sweets shop, La Newyorkina, a time or two. Unfortunately, her shop has closed but thankfully you can still order her incredible ice cream, paletas, and churros online!

CocoAndré Chocolatier
cocoandre.com/

In the very same Dallas neighborhood where my husband grew up sits the most delicious chocolate shop and horchateria you will ever visit. Chocolatier Andrea Pedraza creates truffles that combine European techniques with Mexican flavors such as Dark Chocolate, Tequila, and Cinnamon; Café con Leche; Mole; and others. They ship their chocolates, but their shop is definitely worth a visit if you are in Dallas.

Rancho Gordo
www.ranchogordo.com

If you are as passionate about beans as I am, you probably already know about Rancho Gordo, the heirloom bean company founded by Steve Sando. The company has achieved a cult following so snagging a bag of beans can be difficult, but they are definitely worth the wait and the hefty price tag.

ACKNOWLEDGMENTS

I took my first photography class in high school and the teacher asked me in that very teacherly way, "So, Kate, what do you want to do when you grow up?" I told him I wanted to cook and write and take photographs. He told me maybe one day I could write a cookbook and shoot the images. From that day to this one I have been working toward this book and I want to thank a few special people who helped me get here.

Some people go to a cabin in the woods or to some far-off locale to write their book in peace and silence. I wrote my book while in quarantine with my two young children and my husband in our less than thousand square-foot home, often shooting images on the same table where they were doing their Zoom meetings and virtual learning. Thank you from the bottom of my heart to my loves, Louisa and Hiro, who kept me laughing the whole way, and to my Armando, I thank God for you every day. You are a true partner. I could literally not have done this or really anything else without you. I love you all so, so much. You are my world.

Thank you to my editor, Thom O'Hearn, and everyone at Quarto for giving me a shot and helping me bring my dream to life.

A big thank-you to my family, who have supported me and nourished my passion for food and cooking. A special thank-you to my uncles, Tim Bause and Martin Checov, for opening your home to me when I was starting out and wanting to live my chef's dream in Napa Valley. You were the catalyst for everything that followed.

I've been lucky enough to have work colleagues who have turned into confidants, cheerleaders, mentors, and the dearest of friends. One in particular I'd like to thank is Aida Mollenkamp. Every door that has been opened for you, you pushed it open wider so I could also go through. I am forever grateful for your friendship.

A ginormous thank-you to all the ¡Hola! Jalapeño readers who have cooked with me over the years, shared your stories, and taught me a thing or two. I can't *wait* for you to cook from this book—we did it!

Most importantly, glory be to God, in you I live and breathe.

ABOUT THE AUTHOR

Kate Ramos is the writer and creator of the Mexican-inspired food blog *¡Hola! Jalapeño*. Ramos spent the first ten years of her career in restaurant kitchens cooking under chefs Cindy Pawlcyn and Anne Rosenzweig, at restaurants in Napa Valley, San Francisco, and New York. After leaving the restaurant world, Ramos moved into food writing and editing at CHOW, where she helped manage the look and feel of the publication's food content. During the span of her editorial career, she has written, tested, and edited thousands of recipes. Kate's work has been featured in *Better Homes & Gardens, Cosmopolitan, Elle, Shape, Parade*, Buzzfeed, My Domaine, and Domino. Find her online at holajalapeno.com.

INDEX